Teaching Literature Inductively

Jerry Sullivan

California State University at Long Beach

John Hurley

Santa Ana College

© Copyright 1982
Canterbury Press
5540 Vista Del Amigo
Anaheim, California 92807

This book is dedicated to the many students and teachers who have convinced us that the question is indeed more enlightening than the answer.

Table of Contents

Introduction

This is a handbook of teaching methods and should be of immediate and practical use to any teacher of literature, newcomer or veteran. Application supersedes theory, as the book's design clearly reveals.

Chapter One briefly clarifies the aims and goals of English teachers. Though offering nothing new, it points out that these aims are more often missed than achieved. In Chapter Two we explain why these goals are often unrealized, and we offer the inductive method as the teaching tool that gets the best results.

Chapter Three and the following chapters show the inductive method at work. We deal with three approaches to induction in each chapter: Improvisation, Interpretation, and Intellectualization. We show how these approaches can be applied to all literary forms with equal effectiveness. These three I's represent three levels of understanding, Improvisation being the easiest, Intellectualization the most difficult. Particular classroom situations determine how far into the process the teacher and students will go. The poems (Chapter 3), short stories (Chapter 4), novels (Chapter 5), and plays (Chapter 6) that we apply our methods to are those quite commonly anthologized in high school and college texts. Availability or accessibility, therefore, will be no problem for the teacher using this book.

Chapters three through six are all independently developed units and need not be covered in order. However, we suggest and advise this order because it represents a sound teaching method. Chapter Three deals with shorter, less complicated forms — poetic narratives and lyrics that provide the student ease of access. Chapter Six, on the other hand, deals with longer, more complicated works, a pair of outstanding American plays. Though familiar, at least by name, they present reading difficulties which will be easier to cope with after the student has gained the valuable experiences provided by chapters three, four, and five.

So by following the recommended order, the teacher is able to exploit the most successful teaching technique of all: proceeding from the simple to the complex. This is all that can be asked of any teacher — to give the student the best possible basis for learning.

Chapter 1

The Real Business of
Teaching Literature

Not too many years ago we published an article in
English Journal (Teaching Literature to Adolescents:
Inoculation or Induction? January, 1973, pp. 49-59) in
which we cited a little-known quote from Robert Frost
which goes as follows:

> I don't want to analyze authors. I want to
> enjoy them. I want the boys in the class to
> enjoy their books because of what's in
> them. Here again, perhaps I am old-
> fashioned. Youth, I believe, should not
> analyze its enjoyments. It should live. It
> doesn't matter what they think Hazlitt
> thought or tried to do in his works; what
> matters is the work, the story, the series of
> incidents. Criticism is the province of age,
> not youth. They'll get to that soon
> enough. Let them build up a friendship
> with the writing world first. One can't
> compare until one knows.[1]

We wish to lead off this book with Frost's sentiments
because they still convey our views with regard to
literature and youth, they are still valid themes many

[1]Robert S. Newdick, "Robert Frost as Teacher of
Literature and Composition," *English Journal,* 25 (Oc-
tober 1936) 632-637.

1

years later, and they influence quite a lot what we have to say. Even better, they justify our approach, our method of teaching literature to young readers. We want teachers to induct students into a friendship with the reading world. We want teachers to encourage them to "look" for things, to snoop, to develop a healthy curiosity.

Too often, they sit in a class day after day, pretending to be critics, mechanically analyzing literature. How would you like to discuss terms like *plot, character, theme,* and *image,* as if you were taking inventory? How would you like to go through a number of stories or poems for the purpose of locating and tagging all the parts? Worse yet, how would you like to answer a series of critical questions at the end of each story or poem without having any attachment to or involvement in the work itself? And even if you could get to know the work well, could you, as a youngster, cover the critical questions with any degree of competence? Of course not! So let's get back to basics.

Years ago, when students studied the classics, they had to fight their way through all kinds of grammatical and syntactical oddities in the literature. Needless to say, these methods ruined all but the very strong, who fell in love with the classics in spite of their tormentors, who were posing as teachers. Fortunately, those punitive methods no longer exist because many fine translations are presently available. Now that the excuse for intellectual gymnastics is gone, students can settle back and enjoy the substance of great literature. So the potential for enjoyment is there. The potential exists, and it need not be limited to a few hardy scholars. Good literature is within everybody's reach.

But the obstacles have not all been removed. Our present situation simply reveals that we have substituted one fault for another. Instead of browbeating them, we are boring them. Instead of forcing them to discover linguistic niceties, we are forcing them to put the labels in the right places as each literary package passes before them. Between yawns the students routinely slap a *plot* stamp here, a *theme* stamp there, a *character* label here, and an *image* tag there. Dante couldn't have devised a more hideous kind of Hell.

Still, as in earlier days, a few rugged souls survive, though many are lost. Too many. The cry is out that virtually nobody is interested in literature. Is it any wonder? But it is not great literature that is driving everyone away. It's simply poor teaching methods, poor techniques. After all, great literature can never change. It can never fail to attract people. That is its virtue and its strength. It survives anything — even the worst teaching. We are the ones who must change. We must change our ways now before we drive even the rugged to despair. We have been losers for too long, so by changing we lose nothing.

And the change is easy to make. All we're asking you to do is swap a lifeless, boring method for a dynamic method, a method that promises total involvement, an involvement that can be both profitable and entertaining, not only for the student but also for the teacher. After all, literature is supposed to be fun. And it is. We know it is. We've been there for a long time. We've made hundreds of discoveries, and we're going to make hundreds more before we put the books away. All we ask you to do is to join us. Come along. Try our method. You'll like it. What's more, you'll like literature even more. Though students may not hail you as their redeemer, we assure you they'll walk away from your class with a more profound love of literature. And if you really consider yourself a dedicated English teacher, you'll recognize this as your primary mission: to induce young people to treasure the most civilized expressions of mankind — great literature.

What we advocate is an inquiry approach, and by this we mean that the teacher and the students get involved together to explore the work's possibilities. Answers are not nearly as important as the questions posed, the problems raised, and the improvisational possibilities that each work presents. Every literary work holds an endless number of exploratory possibilities, and because it does, it offers numerous opportunities for discoveries. Students who are constantly making discoveries, finding out for themselves what is useful, enjoyable, and worth retaining, rather than being told what is there, are the students who will come back looking for more. After all, the real business of literature study is to arouse (not implant) interest in the human condition, to refine sensibilities, to alert people to the artistry involved, to cause them to consider man in the universal sense, and to expose them to the finest expression of the cumulative wisdom of civilized society. These goals are not easily attainable and surely not within reach in three or four years of high school or in introductory appreciation of literature courses in college. To suggest that they are is foolish. To try to accomplish them is absurd. Yet we do this. We try to cram, push, stuff, and force-feed literary art into young people as if we were handling so many cans of baby food. We try to win instant devotees and to develop overnight critics, forgetting, as Frost suggests, that the hard work of analysis is something better left to maturer minds and to the accumulation of many, many experiences, even many years of experiences.

Isn't it far better to try to hook young people for just a few years, to get them involved, interested, to give them a taste of what is good and send them away looking for more of the same? Isn't it better to leave them wondering if there is more available somewhere else? Isn't this the ideal attitude, the way students should feel when they leave school? What often happens, however, is that they leave hoping they never have to take any more of that "crap." There have been far better names for literature, to be sure, but few have been devised by students. This kind of student reaction is commonplace evidence that many teachers have apparently worked hard but have only succeeded in turning youngsters off.

Now we contend that the inquiry approach will eliminate this antagonism and that it will do much more. Students will leave school remembering, not the names of heroes or the titles of a dozen stories or the names of characters who seem to fit nowhere. They will leave remembering that they have met many people who encountered many problems which they either overcame or did not. They will leave remembering the triumphs and tragedies, the moments of glory, despair, bliss, embarrassment, pride, jealousy. They will leave remembering that somewhere else, either in some other school or in some other book, another human being is considering another problem and that his predicament is probably worth looking in on. And because they have already been there before, they may want to be there again. That's what we feel the inquiry approach will do: keep them coming back.

Chapter 2

The Inductive Process in Action

We apply a system of inquiry that has served very well in leading our students to a careful examination of a literary work's meaning via the question-asking process. In fact, the questions for the various works treated in the following chapters are a result of classroom projects in which prospective teachers and in-service teachers addressed themselves to a work of literature using the inquiry method discussed in this chapter. We call this system of inquiry the inductive/intuitive process, and we have settled upon three ways to explore it. We call the three approaches the Improvisational, Interpretive, and Intellectual methods of inquiry.

THE IMPROVISATIONAL METHOD

And we'll begin here with a discussion of improvisation as a legitimate method of inquiry. The word "improvisation" is often defined as something done off-hand, something spontaneous, a spur-of-the-moment act, and in these senses the word is quite commonly understood. What often happens is that some person, event, situation, perhaps even a literary work, stimulates or inspires immediate action. In another sense, however, improvisation can simply mean making the best of available materials, and although this activity can be immediate, or spontaneous, it can also be delayed, or deliberate. We want to consider improvisation both ways: the immediate/spontaneous and the delayed/deliberate.

To be sure, on-the-spot improvising sometimes works beautifully. To have a Richard Cory sitting in the corner sulking, considering the great tragic act that will end his life, trying to make a final decision on being or not being — this would make a great scene. Or to have a Richard jauntily stroll through the room as the crowd, sitting humbly on the floor, gapes at him in envy and admiration would be equally effective. And to have students work on mannerisms for both the envied and the envious would be great. But there is as much to be said for studied improvisation. For example, using the facts of the poem, a student could write a brief prose account of Richard Cory's suicide. Or a student could prepare a list of questions concerning Richard's suicide in an effort to determine why he shot himself. Another student could prepare a list of tentative answers independently, as could any other members of the class. Those interested in the motives for or the act of suicide will get involved with little prompting. Other students could check out various suicides by way of *Reader's Guide* or the *New York Times Index* to determine how Richard's was similar to or different from countless other suicides.

Such exploration of literary materials can yield insights of all kinds — practical, moral, emotional, intellectual. The kind and degree of such insights are limited only by the lack of determination, ambition, and industry of the teacher. The teacher who is willing to explore the improvisational potential of literature will be amply rewarded. So will his students.

For the literary works treated in this book, we have included numerous improvisational activities that can be handled by individuals or groups. Some activities work best as creative entry to a study of the work while others work well as a form of creative exit, what we call a consolidation, or capping off, feature. The point to be kept in mind, however, is that these are not activities that emerge as busy work. Rather, they provide a commonsense way of posing questions that bring young people to a greater awareness of the value of a literary work.

Improvisational questions should provide situations and ideas, tangential to the work being studied, which involve students in either a dramatic or a creative way. We don't know what students may create or how they may react. We don't know what questions they will provide, nor do we really care. What we do know is that they will pose the questions that are obviously important to them. Does not anyone who reacts to life in a creative manner do the same? Let students play the part of maker, of artist, for awhile and some of the unanswerables concerning a work of art and its maker might, though still unanswerable, be pleasant to think about. The process can be interesting and absorbing and not half as frustrating as playing the game of always asking why somebody did something so many years ago. If we really knew for sure, would it lessen or heighten our appreciation of the work of art? When the reason for being becomes more important than the art object itself, you no longer deal with a work of art. You deal with gimmickry. You are getting away from the art object itself and focusing on other things calculated to draw attention but not necessarily to make one understand the work any better.

We feel that playing with art's unanswerables is far more fun and far more instructive than knowing all about gimmicks, just as we feel that questions are more important than answers. A meaningful life is a life of searching, not a life which is neatly summarized and analyzed in twenty to one hundred short answers. The students will reveal just how meaningful and instructive art and life can be if given the chance. So give it to them.

The following, general questions led us to the particular improvisational ideas that you find in chapters 3 through 6, and we are convinced that they will do the same for you.

1. Which scenes or incidents in the literary work suggest a dramatic means for involving the students in the experience of the work, i.e., role playing? In "Stopping by Woods on a Snowy Evening," for instance, have one student portray the owner of the woods and another the speaker in the poem. Have the students engage in the dialogue they think would ensue at the meeting of the two in the woods.

2. What kinds of dramatic situations at work in the lives of your students could you create that would better prepare students for imaginative entry

into this particular work? In other words, what in your students' lives is happening that corresponds to something similar in the poem or story to be read or discussed? For example, with the novel *To Kill a Mockingbird*, set up a classroom court scene, but reverse the circumstances of the trial, having a white man attacking a black girl and being judged by an all-black jury. Student creations here should lead to some very interesting insights and implications.

3. What activities (written or oral) does the work suggest that might serve well as a kind of creative exit from the work, a summarizing, consolidating, capping off feature? For example, if you were a servant hoping to benefit from years of service, how would Richard Cory's suicide affect you?

THE INTERPRETIVE METHOD

From creative and reactive improvisation, it seems only a logical step to turn student attention to interpretive inquiry, where you and they attempt to get a meaning of the work itself. You will be surprised at how much and how well the improvisational approach warms students up to a serious discussion of the central meaning of the work itself. The interpretive questions are designed to arouse curiosity by moving the reader gradually from a simple to a complex discussion of meaning, or from a discussion of one meaning to a discussion of many. For example, a teacher trying to deal with questions of character may start out with a simple question about stereotypes. Is Richard Cory a commonly portrayed movie character or television character? Are such people real-life people or just products of fiction? Is his kind of behavior "normal," understandable, acceptable? With regard to setting, why are a lottery, a common twentieth century happening, and the drawing in the story "The Lottery" incompatible? Would a "death" lottery be permitted by law? Could you hold one in your city today? If so, would you show up? What is real — stonings, drawings, traditional events? What is unreal — attitudes, reactions of people, the combination of activities? In dealing with structure and/or form, you could, for instance, ask of "The Lottery," who or where is the central character? Can you find one? Who has the leading part? Or is there a leading role? Considering image and symbol, does the "black box" motif serve to remind you of anything ominous in "The Lottery"? How about the stoning? How about the ritual itself, the blind adherence to it? Consider language, a key element that arouses interesting interpretive questions. For example, is the language chatty, conventional, ironic, figurative, ambiguous, connotative?

The particular points of analysis and the descriptions listed above (and all those on interpretive inquiry in Chapters 3-6) were triggered by these general questions:

1. What questions of character does the work pose (archetypes, stereotypes, believable, unbelievable)?
2. What questions of setting does the work pose (realistic, fantastic, absurd)?
3. What technical questions does the work pose, i.e.
   A. Structure and form?
   B. Image and symbol?
   C. Theme?
   D. Language?

THE INTELLECTUAL METHOD

From improvising to interpreting, we now move to intellectualizing, the final and highest level of inquiry in our process. The intellectual inquiry provides for group interaction, and many of the questions work concomitantly with the interpretive questions. The intellectual questions should elicit from the students responses of a particular and a universal nature. They are intended to get students involved in both the literature and the meaning of their own lives. They should provide for inquiry if they provoke interesting, controversial, intellectual, or, more precisely, thinking questions. They are leading questions, for the most part, but the art of the teacher lies in his/her ability to provide leading questions that move the student to involvement and inquiry — to meaningful interaction. Where a question leads depends on both teacher and student and their prowess for generating more questions that relate to the literary work under discussion. Where the discussion ends may be anywhere, maybe the dismissal bell, but the crucial process of inquisitive thinking should be served, whatever way. The following general questions led the way to the particular questions listed for the various selections offered in chapters 3 through 6:

1. What personal questions does the work pose, i.e., questions that prompt students to examine their feelings, emotions, intuitions, beliefs, values?
2. What kinds of questions would you ask that move students, through inquiry, to self discovery? Keep in mind how the questions might stimulate student questions (and the kinds of questions student questions might provoke).
3. What kinds of questions might assist the student to better understand and appreciate the order and meaning of his existence?
4. How might your questions cause students to
   A. adopt a self-satisfying identity?
   B. cope with loneliness and alienation?
   C. comprehend and interpret man's humanity and inhumanity?

To sum up now, we would like to comment for a moment on the question-asking process we ask you to consider as you prepare works of literature for discussion with your students. We feel that our three-part process of inquiry and the general questions we propose in each process work quite well in leading the inquisitive teacher to the particular kinds of questions found in the following chapters. The general questions we present as a process of inquiry don't always lead you to particular questions that induce a critical, scientific interpretation of a literary work. But we think the discussions which evolve from involved student response go a long way in helping students experience a literary work's significance. The kinds of questions we're proposing stimulate the particular kinds of questions about a work of literature that help young readers become more aware of the relationship between learning and growth. We think they may help adolescents realize that in some ways they are unique in the way they perceive the world. They may acquire empathy by getting in touch with their own feelings and by experiencing the feelings of others. We think if you stress that many of the questions don't have answers, that *most* don't have right answers, that often the answer to a question is another question, you might ultimately teach students how to learn. At least they may become more comfortable with *not* knowing an answer — or with knowing that their answer is subject to change. And young people who are open to changing their answers will not be afraid to ask questions.

In the following four chapters you will find carefully prepared questions that both reveal and demonstrate our method of inquiry. The questions have been applied to works most commonly studied in school. We have selected works from the basic genres (poetry, short story, novel, drama), the staples of literary study in junior high school, senior high school, and even college. Many of the works have been among the most widely read and studied pieces of literature in the schools for years. Others represent our biases, our way of saying that such and such a work belongs in literary study for intellectual, cultural, or just plain enlightening reasons.

What is more important, though, is that the various works treated present the kinds of questions that trigger involved, continuing responsiveness. The questions are not necessarily exhaustive, but they are complete enough to get both teacher and students actively involved in the work, prompting student reaction and interaction. They are questions most students can respond to (not just a few top students), and they are questions students can react to, for the most part, without fear of penalty and embarrassment. Furthermore, they are arranged and designed to permit maximum flexibility, variety, and freedom. The improvisational ideas provide enough variety so that nearly all students can relate to one situation or another and experience the thrill of creative drama that may lend insights into literature that many of us have never dreamed of.

Chapter 3

The Inquiry Method Applied: Poems

In this chapter we have provided improvisational situations and ideas, as well as various interpretive and intellectual questions, for these five poems in this order:

These poems are quite readily available in most anthologies that teachers have at their disposal, and they are most commonly read and studied in junior high or high school, even junior college. With the possible exception of "In Just—," they have been staples in the literature curriculum for years and years. The Cummings' poem is a personal bias. We feel it is a precious one to use with young people and really commands inclusion.

Stopping by Woods on a Snowy Evening

—Robert Frost

Improvisations

1. Close your eyes and picture yourself alone with only some animal as a companion. You are looking at a natural scene. On a piece of paper write down where you are and what animal is with you. Close your eyes again and put yourself as much as possible into the picture you see of yourself and the animal in your mind. As thoughts come to you as you look at the scene, write them down. What, for example, do you think about as you look at the ocean or the mountains or the fields — the natural scene you find yourself in? How does the animal react to you? When you have jotted down your thoughts, go on to wherever you could have been headed before you stopped here. How do you feel about leaving where you are? Would you prefer to stay where you are? If you had not been directed to leave, would you have stayed or would you have moved on anyway? What would have happened had you stayed? Why did you choose to stay? For those who decided to leave, why did you? What compelled you to move on? (Creative entry)

2. Role playing: Have one student portray the owner of

the woods and another the speaker in the poem. Have the students engage in the dialogue they think would ensue at the meeting of the two at the woods. (Creative entry)

3. Imagine you are a high-powered business executive, deeply entrenched in the "rat race." Suddenly you stop what you're doing to watch the rain fall. What does your secretary do when she sees you staring out the window? What does your boss say? How do you react to these two people? (Creative entry)

4. You have just gotten a job that you'll be able to keep for the rest of the time you're in school, one that could become a good, full-time position for you once you graduate. You must be ready to begin work in two weeks to replace employees as they go on vacation. A friend of yours calls you the next day to ask you to spend the summer working with him/her at his/her uncle's dude ranch in Wyoming, something you would really enjoy doing. What will you do — take the job you said you would, or give it up for a summer in Wyoming? What must you take into consideration as you make your final decision? What kind of advice would your friend give you? Your parents? The man who has just hired you? (These last three situations could be dramatized as role-playing situations and could be used either as creative entry or creative exit.)

Interpretive Inquiry

1. Whom do the woods belong to? Does the owner ever stop "to watch his woods fill up with snow"? What

does it matter to the narrator of the poem about who owns the woods? What pleasure does the narrator take from the owner's not knowing someone is enjoying his woods? In what way is the narrator also the owner of the woods?

2. People often misquote the title of this poem to read, "Stopping by *the* Woods on a Snowy Evening." Why do you think Frost entitled the poem "Stopping by Woods..." rather than "Stopping by *the* Woods..."? What difference does the omission of "the" make in the title, or does it make a difference at all? Does the poet stop here often, or do you think this is the first time he has ever stopped here? Had he intended to stop?

3. What kind of human characteristics does the narrator give the horse? Why does the horse react to stopping with no farmhouse nearby? What kind of "mistake" does he think his driver has made? To make stopping seem more irrational and lacking in good sense, what details does Frost use to emphasize how bad the time and place are for stopping? In what physical danger is the narrator if he stays longer to watch the woods? Why is it safer to stop with a farmhouse nearby? For all of his human characteristics, the horse differs from the man. What is the man doing when he stops to see the woods that the horse cannot do?

4. How would you describe the sound of "easy wind and downy flake"? Is this sound in any way like that of the harness bells? If not, how is it different? What tone does the wind create in the poem?

5. During what time of year does the "darkest evening" come? How are the woods dark? The poet observes the woods and finds them "lovely, dark and deep." If he were to go walking in the woods this particular night, how might he also describe the woods? In other words, what is the difference between looking at the woods and actually going into them?

6. What change comes over the narrator when he says, "But I have promises to keep"? Why does he repeat the line, "And miles to go before I sleep"? What kind of sleep is the poet talking about? Is he merely tired?

7. If you read the poem on a literal level, that is, just as it is written, it describes an incident that happened to a person one winter night. If, however, you go beneath the surface to the figurative level, some words take on new meaning. What might the woods represent or mean to the narrator? What could the narrator see there that would make him want to stay? What do the words "promises," "miles," and "sleep" mean figuratively? What does the repetition of line 15 say about the narrator's state of mind as he leaves the woods?

8. What sort of language does Frost use to express his ideas here? Is it poetic? Look at the first stanza. How do you *expect* the four lines to rhyme? With what other lines does line 3 rhyme? Line 7? Line 11? Why might Frost have used such a complicated rhyme scheme in a poem that has simple, conversational language?

Intellectual Inquiry

1. If this poem took place on a clear, starry night, would the poem take on a different meaning? What might that be? Are our feelings about life and/or death any different during the day that they are at night? Have you ever watched "woods fill up with snow," or the sky fill up with sun, or the streets fill up with rain? How does weather affect your mood, personality, or thoughts?

2. If you stopped in woods like these, would you be thinking thoughts about life or thoughts about death? How can snow and dark woods bring on thoughts of death? Would those thoughts of death be peaceful or frightening? Why?

3. Why are natural beauties — sunsets, scenery in parks, untouched snow — so appealing to all people? Why does observing them often bring on contemplation or daydreaming in most of us? Where can beauty be found in an urban or suburban environment? Does that kind of beauty also lead one to contemplation?

4. What is the difference between owning something and really knowing it? Is it possible to possess something by knowing it but not owning it? In what way, for example, are visitors to an art museum the owners of the art they see? When does a book become yours — when you buy it or when you read it?

5. What kinds of responsibilities do you have to yourself? To others? What kinds of situations draw you to them and away from your responsibilities?

What practicalities of living bring you back to reality and remind you of your duties and responsibilities? What consequences do you face when you give in to the lure of the "woods" and forget about your "promises"? Do we ever need to stop by woods from time to time, or must we always be aware of our duties?

6. Do you think there is any place in the world where you would be free of responsibility? Is responsibility always a burden or can it ever be a pleasure? What pleasures can come from taking on responsibilities? How do you feel when an adult does not trust you to be responsible, or will not give you responsibilities? Is it more fun to feel carefree than to have things you must do?

7. What would you do if you felt you had no more promises to keep and no more miles to go before you sleep? Is that a condition of old age? Is it possible to feel that way when you are young (why do so many teenagers commit suicide, for instance)?

Richard Cory

— Edwin Arlington Robinson

Improvisations

1. Have prepared four role descriptions — one snobbish, uncharitable rich; one sympathetic, generous rich; one greedy, bitter poor; and one accepting but envious poor. Have class count off (one, two, three, four, one, etc.), then divide into four

equal groups. Quickly pick four group leaders and hand each a role description sheet. Have the four groups arrange their chairs in tight circles in the four corners of the room. Explain that you are not saying that all rich and poor people fit into these four categories, but that you are asking them to temporarily assume a rigid identity and to maintain it during this assignment. Possibilities for role descriptions:

A. *snobbish, uncharitable rich* — You are rich people, members of the upper social crust. You are surrounded by poverty. You know that while you're eating filet mignon for dinner, most of the poor people around are lucky to have bread. You live alone, eat alone, and share your wealth with nobody. Why should you? Your own company is the best to be had, anyway. Besides, if you shared, *you* wouldn't have as much as you do now, and wouldn't *that* be foolish? As a group, extend this description. Have a group member record your extensions. For example, how do you feel about charity — about trust between people — about love of mankind?

B. *Sympathetic, generous rich* — You are rich people, members of the upper social crust. You are surrounded by poverty, which depresses you. You know that all around you are people struggling just to eat once a day. You have a pretty good idea from the way poor people act around you that some envy you and some hate you. You can *feel* their envy and you know you are part of

24

what motivates their envious greed. You give to charities, but those you see on the street don't know this. As a group, extend this description. Have a group member record your extensions. For example, how do you treat poor people on the street who stare at you? It is considered rude to stare. Do you behave rudely to them to get even?

C. *Greedy, bitter poor* — You are poor people, members of the lowest social caste. Your parents were poor, and your children will be poor, but you cannot do anything about this. Rich people *make you sick*. They're so flaunting, so superior, yet so soft and weak. They probably eat filet mignon every night for dinner, while you eat beans and stale bread, and not very much of that either. When you see a rich person walk by, you think, "Just that silk scarf she's wearing must have cost more than my whole outfit," or, "That's the tenth different pair of shoes I've seen him in this last year, and I don't have one good pair." If you could steal from him, you would. People who have so much must be happy and content all the time. *You* should have been born rich. *You* would've known how to enjoy it — to get the best out of life — good food, rich clothes, the most expensive car there is, etc. As a group, extend this description. Have a group member record your extensions. For example, how would you react if you heard that one of the richest men in the city was an unhappy person?

D. *Accepting but envious poor* — You are poor people, members of the lowest social caste. Your parents were poor and your children will be poor, but you cannot do anything about it. You wish you could, but you see the futility in even trying to change things. So you keep on struggling to eat. One day, maybe you'll get ahead, provide more for your family. When you see rich people on the street, you envy them. They have so much — they *must* be happy. You think, "If only I were he and what he has!" You and your family could certainly be happy if you had even one-tenth of what he has. But at least you have each other, you realize. As a group, extend this description. Have a group member record your extensions. For example, in your present condition, what can you do to better your children's lives and yours?

Give groups 45 minutes (remainder of class time) to discuss respective roles and extend role descriptions. Treat this assignment seriously. Require a legible list of extensions from each group by the end of the period. The next day, return the lists and have either the leaders you chose or the students who have taken over as natural leaders sit in front of the class in desks facing one another. Sticking closely to the assigned roles, the leaders should confront each other, thoroughly expressing their group's beliefs and prejudices. This should result in a more thorough insight into the lack of understanding between groups, especially social levels, and provide a creative entry into Robinson's "Richard Cory."

2. Imagine you are a servant in Richard Cory's household. You know what a fine house he lives in and what expensive possessions he owns. From the little you have seen of him, he's given the impression he is a reasonably happy, friendly man who happens to be quite wealthy. You are at home and have just heard a rumor that he has killed himself. React to this news (a good classroom oral activity or a good writing activity as a creative exit from the poem).
3. Using the facts given in the poem, write a short prose account of Richard Cory's suicide.

Interpretive Inquiry

1. Richard Cory was "a gentleman from sole to crown," not head to toe. Why do you think Robinson used the work "crown," besides the fact that it rhymes with "town"?
2. What does Robinson mean in line 5 when he says Richard Cory was "always quietly arrayed"? Why did he choose those particular words to tell the reader Richard Cory dressed well?
3. Why did Richard Cory "flutter pulses" when he said "Good-morning"?
4. Why does the speaker say (in line 11) "we *thought* that he was everything to make us wish that we were in his place"?
5. What does the speaker mean in line 14 by "cursed the bread"?
6. What light did "we" wait for — line 13?
7. What does Robinson mean to tell his readers in line 6 by saying Richard Cory "was always human when he talked"?

8. Robinson uses several words which suggest that Richard Cory was king-like. What are some of these words?

9. Why was it on "one *calm* summer night" that Richard Cory killed himself? What is Robinson implying here?

Intellectual Inquiry

1. What do you think made Richard Cory kill himself? What specific reasons can you imagine for him to do such a thing?

2. Does this poem say that there are differences between apearance and reality? Briefly explain how Robinson shows this in "Richard Cory." (Tell what Richard Cory's obvious social appearance is, contrasted with what his reality must have been.)

3. Was Richard Cory's suicide an act of total cowardice? Or, was he noble?

4. What does this poem say about lack of understanding between social groups?

5. What feeling did you have after reading this poem? Were you shocked, sad, philosophical? Did you feel empathy for Richard Cory and for others like him, who are caught between public opinion and inner turmoil?

6. Do you know anybody who is rich in material possessions — has a nice car, nice clothes, enough money to buy almost everything he wants — but who you suspect is unhappy? Explain why you think this person is not happy. (What could be lacking in his life?)

7. Have you ever wished you were in another person's place — that you could actually *be* that person? Why would you want to be in another's place? Would it be worth it to give up your own identity, your own self — the person you are and could become?
8. Do you ever think, "When I get this or that (object), then I will be happy"?
9. The poor people "cursed the bread" because it is all they have to eat and they're tired of it. It is, however, life sustaining. Have you ever "cursed" something you have because it is not as good as what someone else has?

10. How do you think a person like Richard Cory feels, walking downtown, probably being stared at, and knowing people are talking about him and envying his wealth?

Reflections on a Gift of Watermelon Pickle Received from a Friend Called Felicity

— John Tobias

Improvisations
1. Students should divide into small groups. Tell them: Pick one of your favorite past experiences and meditate upon it. Recall it as vividly as you can. Where are you? How do you feel? What do you see, smell, hear, etc.? Now come back for a few minutes.

Become aware of your present surroundings and the people around your. Tell your group members how you are feeling. Do you want to go back? Can you experience the past as vividly as the present? Have you focused on some aspects of your experience more than others? Why do you think you do this? If you want to share your experience with your group, describe it until they feel they are with you. Do you think this is what a writer does, or a painter?

2. A group of "Older, wiser" students tries to convince a younger group of "believers" that Santa Claus doesn't exist. Remember that both groups are equally convinced that they are right. What evidence will the "older" students use? How will the "younger" ones defend their belief? Could we say that Santa Claus is just as real to the "believers" as his non-existence is to the "older students"? How does new information change our view of what is real?

3. You are eating watermelon pickle with the speaker when he begins to talk about that summer when watermelons ruled. How does he seem to be feeling (student will need to interpret the speaker's tone)? How do you respond to him? Tell him how you feel about what he is saying.

4. You and your friends are stealing cigarette butts from "family ashtrays." Suddenly your mother walks in and asks what you want them for. What will you tell her?

5. Students could act out the scene of eating the "thick pink imperial slices" of watermelon, or have an imaginary black-bullet-seed-fight. Students in the au-

30

dience (newspaper reporters) could write "factual" accounts of what they saw. These reports should be compared. Why is each account different? Which of these accounts is more "real"? What really happened?

6. Imagine that this is the last day of a week's vacation in the mountains. You've had a great week, you won't get back for awhile, and you really hate to go, but tomorrow you've got to be back in Los Angeles. Tell your friends what you most want to do today before you pack up camp. What do we do when we must (but don't want to) leave or say good-bye or stop what we're doing?

Interpretive Inquiry

1. What are "unicorns"? Where do "unicorns" live? What might "unicorns" symbolize? When are unicorns "still possible"?
2. What are the "softening effects/Of civilization"? Can you find any examples of them in the poem?
3. Why might that summer "never have been at all"? Why has it "become more real/ Than the one that was"? Do you think this expresses a truth about the way we perceive or remember our experiences?
4. Why does John Tobias say "hungers" rather than "hunger"?
5. Why have the once "limitless" bites become fewer now? How have the bites changed? What does this tell us about the speaker?
6. How is the change in the form of the watermelon related to the change in the way the speaker eats the

watermelon? Can you see more than one level of meaning in the watermelon? What could the watermelon symbolize?

7. How does Tobias use form to give a feeling of bullet seeds spit out in rapid fire? Why do you think be puts "Hollowed out...In family ashtrays" in parentheses?

8. Why do you think the speaker's friend is called Felicity? What does "felicity" mean? Does this word choice make the poem more meaningful? Explain.

9. John Tobias has just taken you on a trust walk through the unknown territory of his poem. At times he made you speed up; at other times you slowed down. How did he do this? Why do you think he did?

10. How old do you think the speaker is now? How old do you think he was that summer when watermelons "ruled"?

11. When John Tobias writes that "the purpose of knees/Was to be skinned," do you think of a boy or a girl? Why do you think so? Would you feel the same way if the author was a Becky or a Martha Tobias? How can we tell the speaker's voice from the author's voice?

12. During that summer the speaker was "far above and away" from these softening effects of civilization. Where is he now? Can you imagine his surroundings?

13. Can you supply the missing word from your own experience: During that summer, _____ ruled?

14. How do you feel about the speaker? What kind of person do you think he is now? Would you like to know him better?

Intellectual Inquiry

1. Can you think of any experiences in your own life which remind you of those John Tobias describes? In what ways are they similar? In what ways different?
2. When do you most feel like getting far away from the "softening effects of civilization"? What modern "conveniences" do you think you could live without?
3. Do you think people might become more careful as they get older? Why might this happen?
4. Do you ever feel that you need a time for reflection? What value could it have for you? What good does it do to look at our past experiences?
5. What "unicorns" are possible for you?
6. What does it mean to grow up? In what ways would you like to grow up? In what ways would you like to stay the way you are now?
7. What experiences in your own life would you like to "preserve"? Why? Are some experiences in your life more meaningful to you now than when they happened? How could you explain this?
8. Do you think we tend to remember good times more than bad ones? Do you think this is desirable?
9. Do you eat watermelon in the same way you approach life? Are you more like a careless gorger or a bit-by-bit slicer?

THE UNKNOWN CITIZEN

W.H. Auden

Improvisations

1. About a week before the poem is discussed, each student will be given a number. He/she will be referred to by number rather than name for one week both by teacher and other students.

2. Students bring to class at least one advertisement (television, magazine, or newspaper) that they believe to be misleading and one advertisment they feel has influenced them. A one-period group discussion should draw out insights into the power of mass media and the games played with marketing analysis (statistics).

3. Have a student (or several) appear before a class committee requesting that his/her number be exchanged for his/her given name (good creative exit from the poem). The student will plead his/her case before the committee (the whole class could serve as committee). The class will decide whether to accept or reject such a request.

Interpretive Inquiry

1. What does "JS/07/M/378" mean? Why does the unknown citizen have a number? Who gave him a number?

2. Because there wasn't any official complaint against the unknown citizen, does that make him a saint? Describe a saint. How is that description different

from the description of the unknown citizen in the poem? Why did Auden call the unknown citizen a saint?

3. In what way did the unknown citizen serve the greater community? Who really did he serve?

4. Why wasn't he odd in his views? If he had been odd in his views, would he have been popular with his mates?

5. What type of newspaper did he read? What type of magazines did he read? What type of books did he read?

6. In what way were his reactions to advertisments normal?

7. Did he have everything necessary to modern man?

8. What were the proper opinions that he held? Where did he get his proper opinions? Did he believe his proper opinions?

9. Why did he go to war if he was for peace?

10. Why didn't he interfere with his children's education? Should he have interfered with his children's education?

11. Was the unknown citizen free? Was he happy? Why is it absurd to ask those questions? Was there anything wrong with the life of the unknown citizen? If anything had been wrong with his life, would he have been heard from?

12. Who was the unknown citizen? Is he still alive today? Where does he live? Describe him today. How does that description differ from the description in the poem.

13. Give one word that describes the unknown citizen.

14. Is the author of this poem serious or is there a hidden meaning - maybe a meaning opposite of what is stated?
15. What is irony?

Intellectual Inquiry

1. The unknown citizen had a number. What number(s) do you have? How would you like to exchange your name for a number?
2. The unknown citizen wasn't odd in his views. Do you know anyone who has odd views? Why are the views of that person odd? Do you think that your views are odd to that person? What standard do you use to decide if a person's views are odd? Do you think that a person should change his views that you consider odd? How do you try to change a person's views that you consider odd? Would you associate with a person whose views you consider odd?
3. The unknown citizen's reactions to advertisements were normal. What are your reactions to advertisements? What are advertisements designed to do? Are you influenced by advertisements? Do you question the information that is contained in advertisements?
4. The unknown citizen had everything necessary to modern man. What do you think is necessary for modern man? What is necessary for you? Are these things necessary, or are your reactions to advertisements normal?
5. The unknown citizen held the proper opinion for the time of the year. Do you think that he changed his

opinion to suit the occasion? Why do you think he did this? Have you ever expressed an opinion that you didn't believe? Why did you do this?

6. Auden does not mention the unknown citizen's religious or political beliefs. Do you think the unknown citizen had religious or political beliefs? Why doesn't Auden mention his religious or political beliefs? What ethical or moral virtues do you think the unknown citizen is lacking?

7. Do you like the unknown citizen? Would you like to become like him? Could you become the unknown citizen? What can you do to prevent becoming one?

In Just

— E. E. Cummings

Improvisations

1. Students are divided into groups of five. One becomes an old man in a shabby brown suit who walks in the park every day. He always has balloons and candy in his pockets for the neighborhood kids. The other students should approach him, showing their reactions to such a man. (They might be fearful, feel sorry for him, come to him for the candy and run, or adore him.) Remember, the other four are *children* . (This will later be related to students' perceptions of the balloon Man.)

2. Pretend you're eight years old, and you don't want to move away from your neighborhood, but your dad changed jobs. Show how you feel before the

move and then afterwards, when you're telling your mom excitedly about the nice kids on your new block. Rattle off their names as quickly as children would, and tell her the games you played together. (Does it sound like what Cummings tried to create in the lines of his poetry? Review how he got the reader to feel as bubbly as the children.)

3. An elderly couply is sitting on a park bench, enjoying the sunshine, and discussing the leisure time that they are grateful for, now that they're retired. Then they see some children playing and suddenly they are back in their own home town, remembering the shopkeeper, the teacher who scolded them, and so on. Students should portray whether they are still content with their retirement, or whether they wish they could turn back the clock.

4. Act out a Greek setting on Olympus, complete with gods and goddesses reveling in their respective duties. *Volunteers* from the class might be best, regarding which "deity" they'd like to be, since some will have more knowledge of this than others. There might be a brief discussion preceding this regarding animal characteristics, cloven hooves, "goatfooted," etc. (Pan must be represented in this!) They should experience "paradise" outside of the concept of youth, and children, exclusively.

Interpretive Inquiry

1. What does "mud-luscious" mean to you? Does it make you feel happy or sad? When do you live in that kind of a world?

2. Is the author talking only about springtime, or is it possible to feel like this any time of the year? Why does he capitalize the J in "Just-spring" and then never use the word again? Do you get a feeling of the passage of time? How?

3. How does the saying, "April showers bring May flowers" tie in with this poem? Can you see a change in our California seasons, or does the whole year seem the same to you? Would your perceptions change if you opened your eyes in a new way to your surroundings?

4. Does it have to rain to make a "puddle-wonderful" world? Is rain mentioned anywhere in the poem? Why not?

5. Why did the author write "eddieandbill" and "bettyandisbel" as one word — without capital letters? Shouldn't names always be capitalized?

6. Look at the poem. What words do you see repeated? ("Far and wee") Are they written the same each time? Can you "hear" a difference in each whistle?

7. Is this more a poem of feeling or thinking? How do you know? Why do you think there aren't any periods used in the poem? Would it have made a difference in your mood if there had been?

8. What images of your childhood does this bring to mind? Did you ever play hop-scotch or jump rope? How does the poem make you hear sounds? What did you hear as you read?

9. Did you like the appearance of the poem? Did you object to the lack of punctuation in it? The irregular spacing? The slant of "the goat-footed" lines? Did

the author's variation add to or detract from the poem for you? In what ways? (Consider mood and subject matter.)

10. Would this be a hard poem for you to share with someone else? Is it a poem you could explain? Would you want to? (or rather savor it yourself?)

11. What could the balloonman represent? Would you call him the main character? Why do you think Cummings describes him first as "little" and "lame," then "queer" and "old," and finally as "goat-footed?" Does a change take place in him — or in the reader? (Growth, spring, etc.)

12. Does the character become more alive to you? Do you feel any different towards him at the end of the poem? Do you ever think of him as being like the Pied Piper? Would you want to follow him? Why? What do you like about him?

13. Does Cummings capitalize the M in balloonMan for a reason at the end? What do you think it could be? Does he seem any more important than he once was? What imagery comes to mind (Pan)? Does that give you any clues? Does this character need a name for you to feel close to him?

14. What setting do you envision for this poem? Where does it take place? Could it be in your neighborhood, or is it never-never land? Does it seem corny, or do you enjoy it? Discuss the time element involved (the season, time covered here, the age group...).

15. Does a child narrate this poem? Study the

vocabulary used. Is it about the world of children, though?

16. What kind of a mood do you think the author was in when he wrote it? Do you think he had a message, or purpose, or did he write it for fun?
17. Is it important that the characters mentioned are not developed much? Who are the real characters in the poem?

Intellectual Inquiry

1. What memories of people came back to you after reading this poem? Were they all happy? Does an experience have to result in personal success for it to be meaningful?
2. Does it take a long time for you to get adjusted to a new situation? Do you have to "warm up" to something before you can get into the swing of things... Does Spring hit you all at once, or do you grow with the season?
3. How much do you think is "fact" in a person's environment, and how much can he improve his situation by his own attitude? Do you think the balloon-man, for instance, could have turned into a sour old man instead?
4. Can you find universal truths in such a small poem, written in so casual a style? Should we say that learning has to be painful to take place? Or is it possible to gain a world of truth in a few choice words from a friend, or an expression from a loved one? What ways do you show your concern for others that you hope will linger in their minds?

5. In life, are you a "balloonman" or a child? Do you see yourself as a giver or a taker? How do you think others see you?

6. Which character do you believe you're most like regarding the way you go through life? The balloonman (or -Man)? Why? Eddie and Bill? (Maybe because they could be seen as playing games and aiming for self-interest — "piracies," etc.) Do you dance through life, like Betty and Isabel — and if so, what kind of a dance best represents you?

7. Do you think it will be hard for you to go through the muck of life and still come out calling it "puddle-wonderful," or "mud-luscious"? Is that unrealistic, knowing yourself? If so, what could be done to improve your attitude?

8. When is "Just- spring" for you?

9. What do you do with yourself when you get so excited that you feel like a balloon about to burst? Could you get that feeling from reading the poem?

10. What does it mean to have "spring fever"? Do you think it's nonsense, or can you identify with it? Do you ever get it? Does the balloonman have it?

11. What things pop into your mind when you think of your favorite season? Are you more influenced by the weather or the people you're with? Can playmates like "eddieandbill" give you a warm feeling even when everything else seems to be going wrong?

12. What "piracies" do you remember as a child? Is that the same as playing pirates and buccaneers, or does it bring more to mind? What good things do

you wish you could steal back from your childhood?

13. Did you get so carried away in your play with others that someone got hurt? When you look back, do you ever wish you could have been more gentle? Do you think children understand the difference between play and reality? — Do adults?

14. Would a "puddle-wonderful" world be inviting to you? Does the way you view puddles make you want to splash happily, or avoid them? If there were a puddle in this room, would you jump into it? If not, what would stop you?

15. How much have you changed from your childhood? Does mud seem dark and dirty now to you, or do you remember times when you loved it? Did mud pies ever cleanse away hurt feelings or smooth over troubled friendships? Is life so simple now? Do you wish it were? Why?

16. What stops you from going back to those days of carefree play? Does "growing up" mean you can't have fun anymore? Do the adults you know have fun, or do they usually take life seriously? — Too seriously?

17. What "balloonmen" have you met in your lifetime? Did they leave you with more than balloons? Did the balloons pop, or did your hopes and happiness stay the same? When's the last time you saw a balloon-man — in real life (like at Disneyland), or symbolically, someone who reminded you of what you pictured? Were you disillusioned?

Chapter 4

The Inquiry Method Applied: Short Stories

In this chapter we have provided improvisational situations and ideas, as well as various interpretive and intellectual questions, for these five short stories in this order:

We think you will agree that these stories are probably among the most widely read short stories in American schools. Furthermore, they are commonly available in most literature textbooks or short story collections for young readers. They are stories that young readers relate to or enjoy, and they are written by authors who have few peers in the short story genre.

The Lottery

-Shirley Jackson

Improvisations

1. Send *seven* students out of the classroom and tell them that upon their return they will be asked to do something, and anyone failing to follow orders will receive an "F" for the day. Place *six* chairs in the front of the room. When the students return, the first order will be to sit on one of the chairs. Note reaction of the scapegoat (the chair-less student).

2. Students might enact a family argument in which the parents insist they are right simply because of the way it was in the "old days," giving no consideration to the changing conditions in society and the changing values of the children. Possible subjects for discussion might be smoking pot, corporal punishment in schools, fighting for one's country -right or wrong, etc.

3. Students might improvise a town-council meeting involving a debate between the older people who want to keep the lottery and the younger ones who wish to abolish it. What arguments might each side present? What compromise(s) might be worked out? The same idea might be used concerning the abolishment of a presentday problem (capital punishment, abortion, whatever) substituted for the lottery idea.

4. Ditto off the New Testament parable of the sower and the interpretation Jesus gives it and read these to the class. Note that in the parable the sower is any

sower; in "The Lottery" the people of the village are any people of any town and Mrs. Hutchinson is any homemaker. Have the students write an interpretation of "The Lottery" in the style of Christ's interpretation of the parable of the sower.

5. The day before assigning the reading of "The Lottery" take about the last ten minutes of the period and discuss the meaning of tradition. The following assignment will be due the day the reading is to be assigned: Have students list things that have become traditions in their own homes and families, and here at their school. Tell them to think about any of these traditions that have changed, or have not changed, so they can discuss examples in class.

6. After the initial discussion of tradition, ask for two or three volunteers. Have one of them question the principal, and the other two question some of the teachers who have been at the school for several years about the kinds of traditions they have had at the school. Find out how many still exist, which ones have been changed, why they have or have not, which ones have been eliminated and why, and then get each of their feelings about these traditions. This will be prepared to share with the entire class.

Interpretive Inquiry

1. Reread the opening paragraph of the story, noting the details Jackson gives. How do these details give a sense of credibility to the story, i.e., how do they trick the reader into believing this is a real village and the lottery a normal event for the village? What

46

other details in the opening section of the story help give a sense of reality to the events about to take place when the lottery begins?

2. The original black box no longer exists, many parts of the ritual have been forgotten, and many changes have taken place in connection with the lottery. Of what significance are these facts? Is there any connection between the loss of the original rituals and the fact that some villages have dropped the practice of holding a lottery and others are considering giving it up? Why do these villagers continue to hold the lottery?

3. Why is it significant that the one part of the lottery ritual the villagers have not forgotten is to use stones? (The author makes this very plain: "Although the villagers had forgotten the ritual and lost the original black box, they still remembered to use stones.") How else might the villagers kill the victim? What would be unsatisfactory about simply shooting the person? Why did everyone need to participate?

4. Why is it significant that the box is black? That it is made up of pieces of the box that preceded it? That, despite its shabbiness, no one wants to make a new one? Why does it have no permanent storage place in between lotteries?

5. What do you know about the character of Mr. Summers, Old Man Warner, Mrs. Dunbar, and Mrs. Hutchinson from the story? Why is there little character interest developed in the story? What effect comes from using characters who are simply

typical, small-town people? What might have changed in the story had someone important in the village drawn the paper with the black spot?

6. What is a scapegoat? Who is the scapegoat in this story? Why does Tessie Hutchinson keep insisting in the end that the lottery isn't "fair"? Did she feel the lottery was unfair when it began? What is gained by having Mrs. Delacroix select the first stone?

7. What is the usual meaning associated with the word *lottery*? What makes the title of this story ironic? Why does the author withhold information about the purpose of the lottery until nearly the end of the story? The atmosphere of the earlier part of "The Lottery" is in direct contrast with that at the end. How would you describe this contrast? What insight does it give about human nature?

8. Is the reaction of Nancy and Bill, Jr. when they find their slips of paper are blank ("both beamed and laughed, turning round to the crowd and holding their slips of paper above their heads") strange? What thoughts do people who have escaped from a fire, for example, have about those who didn't? Is this a normal human reaction to someone else's distress?

9. Old Man Warner saw the lottery as necessary and vital to the village. What might he represent?

10. The Adamses questioned the necessity of the lottery. What might they represent?

Intellectual Inquiry

1. What traditions from the past do we cling to for

which we don't remember the reasons or origins?

2. Why do people often think that just because something was good in the past, it will be that way for all time? What are some of the things your parents think were better in the "old days"? What things do you think were better in the past?

3. Do you think many mothers and fathers would be relieved that they "won" the lottery so that their children could be spared? What experiences have you had or heard about in which one person gives his life for another? Is there any evidence of this kind of courage in this story?

4. What superstitions do you believe in? Do superstitions play a beneficial or harmful role in people's lives?

5. Why was it important for the man to draw the lot for the family? Do men and women in our society play certain roles solely because of tradition? What examples can you think of? What changes in male/female roles do you think would contribute to better human relations? What traditional roles do men and women have which are worth keeping?

6. Do you think that people are basically savage or kind? Do we cover up our bestiality with sweetness or are we born good people who become corrupted in some ways by society?

7. Who are the scapegoats in today's society? Have there been situations in which you felt you were a scapegoat?

8. Does the lottery compare to maybe a "rain dance"? What do you think would happen to the corn if they

stopped the lottery? Why?

9. How many times have you found yourself going along with something even if it might hurt another human being? What kinds of feelings did you experience?

10. In the animal kingdom, "survival of the fittest" is an inborn characteristic. Do these same instincts appear in man in our "civilized" society?

Paul's Case

-Willa Cather

Improvisations

1. A student will appear before a faculty group (peers in class) to request re-admission to school after a suspension for "disorder and impertinence." The faculty will have to indicate what exactly the student has done wrong and either accept or reject the request.

2. Students will role play a father-son situation (or a mother-daughter situation) where the father (mother) wants his son (daughter) to be like someone else. The students should determine the characteristics of the "model" person, and the son (daughter) will then reject and/or pacify the parent's wishes. A follow-up discussion should cover how this situation parallels Paul's, and the consequences which often follow in real life.

3. Students will act out each of the following characters' reactions to and explanations of Paul's

suicide: a) Paul's father; b) Paul's English teacher; c) Paul's drawing master; d) Charley Edwards; d) a neighbor from Cordelia Street.

4. Students pick some person they fantasize about and then try to convince other students (by lying) that the fantasy is real. Example: A girl fantasizes about being asked out by the most popular boy in the school for the biggest dance of the year. Then, when she convinces students that the date is real, they find out the most popular boy was at the dance with someone else, and they demand an explanation from the student who lied. The student then must come up with some answer for the change of dates.

Interpretive Inquiry

1. What is Paul's temperament? How does it show in the way he treats his teachers? In his attitude toward the people he seats at Carnegie Hall? Why does Paul feel so strongly that his English teacher has no right to sit downstairs during the concert at Carnegie Hall?

2. Paul's ushering at Carnegie is described as "orgies of living" that were followed by "the physical depression which follows a debauch." Why does Paul consider concerts and his visits to the theater "living," while real life isn't living at all? What are his physical reactions after these "orgies"?

3. Paul lies to everyone — his teachers, his classmates, his father — and keeps getting caught at it. Since it really hurts no one but Paul, is it more like telling "white" lies, or does his lying indicate there is

something seriously wrong with him? In what ways does the lying affect him? What are the flaws in Paul's egocentric view of the world, a view that causes him to lie?

4. What class of people lives on Cordelia Street? Is it a lower-, middle-, or upper-class neighborhood? Cather describes the men as "the burghers of Cordelia Street." What does the term "burgher" imply about them? In what respects were the people on the street alike?

5. How did Paul conform to the expectations of his family and neighbors? (He certainly is not the rebellious child we think of today who refuses to conform in all ways.)

6. How does Paul's view of beauty differ from that of an artist (poet, painter, musician)? How does the beauty of the music he hears at Carnegie or the art in the picture gallery there affect him? How does be appreciate it? Since Cather says an element of artificiality is necessary in Paul's conception of beauty, how are the fresh flowers he insists on having in his hotel room in New York artificial?

7. Why did Paul feel no need to lie in New York? What is the "purple" Paul wore that no one questioned?

8. Did Paul expect to be discovered in New York? Had he not been, would he have returned home when his money ran out?

9. Why was the method of suicide Paul chose appropriate for the life he had dreamed about living? Why did he decide that shooting himself was inappropriate?

10. Paul had enjoyed hearing stories about places like Venice, Monte Carlo, and the Mediterranean. Before he dies, Paul thinks of the Adriatic Sea and of the Algerian sands; these are to him "the vastness of what he had left undone." Why does he think of faraway places just before he dies? Do these thoughts indicate that Paul is finally in touch with reality?

Intellectual Inquiry

1. Paul did not conform to the attitudes or behavior of his fellow classmates, nor did he follow accepted behavior in the classroom. Do you think a person who does not fit in at school wants to be unusual or different? Does your behavior perhaps seem strange to that person? Do you like people who have different interests from yourself or your friends? Do you think a person should try to change his interests and attitudes to conform to yours? How do you try to change a person's attitudes that you consider strange? How do your teachers try to change a person's attitudes that they consider strange or inappropriate?

2. Paul became accustomed to lying in order to get away from unpleasant situations. Do you know anyone who lies often to relieve pressures in his home or school life? Do you ever lie in order to avoid hassles or to get your own way? Have you ever lied when you really didn't want to? Do people or situations ever put you in a position where you feel forced to lie? Has lying ever helped you solve a pro-

blem or escape an unpleasant situation? Does lying ever affect you physically, i.e., do you get sick, feel uneasy, get ulcers?

3. Throughout the story, Cather describes Paul as "losing himself" or escaping into the colorful world of Carnegie Hall or New York. Did Paul merely "lose himself" in something he enjoyed or did the excitement of his fantasies take over his entire life? Do you ever lose yourself in an activity (sports, dancing, reading) or a surrounding (the beach, a movie theatre, a party) which you enjoy very much? What is the difference, then, between "losing yourself" in actually doing something and "losing yourself" in pretending to be something you are not? Is fantasizing ever justifiable? Does it ever serve any good purpose?

4. Does Paul have a realistic image of himself? Does he ever slip out of the role he imagines he is playing? In dealing with different people (teachers, parents, friends, siblings), do you ever play a role that is very different from what you really are? How important is it to have a realistic self-image?

5. Cather gives the reader very few descriptions of what Paul thinks of himself. Do you think Paul respects himself? Other people? Do other people respect Paul? Why is it sometimes difficult to like and respect other people if you are not happy with yourself?

6. Why do you suppose that the members of the stock company agree with Paul's father and teachers "that Paul's was a bad case"? What did Paul have a "bad

case" of? How did each of the people in Paul's life — his father, his teachers, Charley Edwards — try to solve his "bad case"? Cather doesn't entitle the story "Paul's Bad Case," but simply "Paul's Case." Is there any other meaning implied in the word *case* besides the one we typically think of when we use the phrase "bad case"?

7. Why did Paul place more importance on material possessions and places than on people? How might his mix-up in values have compounded his confusion, fears, and unhappiness? Was he alone to blame for his values? How could Paul's father or neighbors have influenced his poor value system? Were they capable of changing it?

8. Is Paul in any way a likeable character? What strengths and weaknesses does he have? What characteristics of Paul are probably in all of us? If we all have some of his flaws, what keeps us from becoming like him?

The Secret Life of Walter Mitty

James Thurber

Improvisations

1. (Oral interpretation) This story can be read or acted out most effectively. For example, try assigning each daydream sequence to different members of the class to read while you read the narration.

2. Ask individual students to assume the characters of Mr. and Mrs. Mitty and put them on the hot seat.

They must remain "in character" as students fire questions at them.

✗ 3. You are giving a cocktail party for Walter Mitty. Explain what celebrities you would invite and why.

✗ 4. You are the casting director for the movie version of "The Secret Life of Walter Mitty." Who would you cast in the parts and why?

writing

5. Explain which of the following gifts (or a different one of your own selection) you would give Walter Mitty for his birthday and why it would be the perfect gift.
   — a case of Cutty Sark
   — 100 shares of IBM
   — a new sports car
   — a vacation in Africa

6. Deliver a eulogy for Walter Mitty including how he died and how good his life was. *or husband*

7. You are Mrs. Mitty. Tell us about the secret life your husband leads.

8. A day or so prior to assigning this story to the class, arrange with one of the more dependable students to utter a word or phrase outloud periodically in class that will be totally out of context with the normal activities. The student could perhaps say, "banana split," or "ice cream cone," or any other thing which will seem like nonsense to the other students in the class. After reading the story, discuss with the class their reactions to this student speaking out in class in this unusual manner.

9. Assign each student to write a paragraph describing a daydream he or she has had. Ask for volunteers to

read their papers. Later, ask the students to write a second paragraph; this one slightly different. Each student is to pick out secretly a member of the class and write what he or she thinks that student might daydream about. The students are not to identify the student about whom they are writing. Based on what they know about the other student, they are to attempt to "dream up" what kinds of daydreams others have.

10. Divide the class into small groups, perhaps three or four to a group, and have them discuss the value or the human need to dream and to have private thoughts. Ask them also to discuss how movies, television, and literature help to answer one's need for dreaming. *thoughtful - bridge*

Interpretive Inquiry

1. How does Mrs. Mitty break into Walter's "secret life"?

2. What is your immediate impression of Mr. and Mrs. Mitty's marital relationship?

3. How does Mrs. Mitty handle Walter? What tone of voice does she use with him?

4. When she orders him to get a pair of overshoes for himself, he replies: "I don't need overshoes." How will he say that? Straight Milquetoast style? Will some of the military bearing of his fantasy world trail over into reality? Will it take time for Commander Mitty to subside into hen-pecked husband with "the roaring of the SN202 through the worst storm in twenty years of Navy flying fading in the

remote, intimate airways of his mind''?

5. The structure takes the form of episodes alternating between the inner and outer experiences of one man. Which kind of experience is given the most space in the story? How does this emphasis help you understand Mitty's personality?

6. Consider the roles Walter Mitty plays in his daydreams. In these, what capabilities and personal qualities does he demonstrate? What impression does he make on others? How do the daydreams contrast with his daily life?

7. What does Mitty reveal about himself when he says, ''We only live once, sergeant . . . Or do we?''

8. How does he show personal insight when he replies to the sergeant's ''It's forty kilometers through hell, sir'' — ''What isn't''?

9. What gives Mitty satisfaction in his last daydream? Compare the last dream with the first. Does the direction of Mitty's fantasies, established by the order of the episodes, tell something important? (In the first, he is the commander who saves a planeful of men; in the last, he is facing the firing squad, comforted only by the pathetic notion that he is ''inscrutable.'') What trend do you see?

10. How long do you think Walter and Mrs. Mitty have been married? Do they have any children? Why aren't we told Mrs. Mitty's first name? Is it of any importance to the story? What is the Mittys' relationship? Do you think they care deeply for one another?

11. How does Mitty's daydream life differ from his real

life? Why does the author use the title, "The Secret Life of Walter Mitty"? From whom is Mitty keeping his life secret? Why do you think he has a secret life?

12. Would this story be as effective if the daydreamer were Mrs. Mitty? Would the story be as funny? Why? Why not?

13. Reread the last paragraph of the story. Focus on the last sentence in particular. Do you think the author has attempted to leave the readers with a sense of hope or hopelessness for Walter Mitty?

Intellectual Inquiry

1. Daydreams can serve as visions in which a normal person sets goals for future action. What purpose do daydreams serve in Mitty's life? What purpose do daydreams serve in your life? Have you ever daydreamed something and then gone out and made it come true?

2. Mitty says, "We only live once, sergeant . . . Or do we?" Do some people have more than one life? Might some people be said never to "live" at all?

3. Although the story was written a number of years ago, would you say that "media" have had an effect on Mitty's life? Could too much television have this effect on someone's life? Is television an escape mechanism? Does television portray a realistic or a fantasy world? Is this necessarily harmful? How regularly do you watch television? Do you know any television addicts? Are there any other escape mechanisms you see people using?

4. Is Walter Mitty bored with the routine of ordinary

living? Is boredom becoming more common among people today? What are some of the common outlets for boredom? How could boredom be dangerous? What do you do when you are bored in class? In the evening? During the holidays? If so many people are bored, how has our culture failed them?

5. In what ways might Mitty feel threatened by a technological culture he can neither understand nor control? Is this feeling unusual in modern man? Do machines ever frustrate you? What does Mitty consider doing to cope with his mechanical maladroitness? Did you ever kick a machine or a toy that wouldn't work right? Are you threatened by the growing uses of computers? Are you afraid of some of the "unplanned" capabilities and thinking capacities computers are rumored to possess? How can man understand or control his technological age?

6. Thurber is said to be a persistent "champion of the male animal." Is it Mrs. Mitty's fault that Walter has so many problems? Do you know anyone with her particular qualities? Do you know any henpecked males? Why does Mrs. Mitty criticize her husband? Could he have really been driving too fast? How would you feel if someone like him were the bread winner in your household? Do you know any couples with qualities similar to the Mittys' where the relationship really works out well? Is Mrs. Mitty a victim of our culture just as much as he is? Would she be less of a bitch if she were more liberated? If she were able to put chains on the tires herself, could

she not take some of the pressure of a mechanical age off her husband? Why doesn't she do the driving? Do the stereotyped roles of man and woman have them both in a trap? Which came first, his daydreams or her nagging?

7. Mitty does not tell his wife what he is thinking. He does tell her, "I was thinking." Why do you think Mitty does not tell his wife what he is thinking about? Do you think that Mitty feels she will not understand, or perhaps laugh at him? Do you sometimes feel that other people will think you odd or funny for your dreams? Do you have anyone who is willing to share his or her dreams with you?

8. In each of his dreams, Mitty is jerked back to reality by some form of authority: his wife, the parking attendant, the policeman. Why do you think the author uses this device?

9. The author has portrayed Mrs. Mitty as an authority figure over Mitty. Why do you think this is so? Is it possible for those who are close to us and love us to still be a figure of authority? Can the use of authority also be seen as a means of showing care and concern?

10. Mitty's rebellion could be likened to a young child throwing a bit of a temper tantrum. Is such behavior typical of human beings when they are being put down? Do you ever find yourself reacting in a similar fashion?

11. Mrs. Mitty makes Walter put on his gloves, but he takes them off after she is gone. What is the author trying to tell us when this happens? Have you ever

done something you were told not to do? How do you react when you are caught? Do you do what Mitty did?

12. Mitty seems able to drive his car, do his shopping, and other routine functions while completely wrapped up in his dream world. Is it possible that some things become so routine to us that we are not required to think about them? Do you ever get in trouble because of something like this?

13. Who is it that Mitty is referring to when he says, "They think they know everything"? Are there people in your life who act as though they know everything? How do you react to such people? Do you ever get the feeling that your parents or your teachers think they know everything?

14. Why does Mitty decide to wear his arm in a sling the next time he has to have the chains taken off the car? Do you ever make excuses for failing to be able to do something? Why does a person feel the need to make such excuses?

15. Why does the author portray Mitty facing a firing squad at the end of the story? What is Mitty's reaction to facing the firing squad? Is he really thinking about having to face something else? Does the author seem to be saying that Mitty is about to face the ultimate challenge, his wife? How do you react when you know that you are in for a really bad time either at home with your parents or at school?

The Fall of the House of Usher

Edgar Allan Poe

Improvisations

1. Arrange for one of the students to plant the seeds of fear in his classmates (perhaps regarding the possibility of a pop quiz). Have him attempt to spread his fear and note how quickly the others become frightened because of his show of nerves. Discuss with the class how the attitude of fear can quickly spread, even without a person being superstitious.

2. Prior to reading "Usher," arrange to have a gloomy color week. Have the students wear dark colors and work in a classroom that is darkened somewhat. At the end of the week ask the students if they noted any change in their moods or dispositions because of the dark colors and surroundings. Were they more depressed? Were they bored or inhibited by the color? Does this have any relation to the fact that rainy days bring on depression?

3. Have an art session. Have the students draw a picture of the human mind in terms of the structure of a house with rooms. Have them compare minds and note the differences in the drawings. Is a person's drawing indicative of his personality? Now let the students draw a picture of an idea. Try a morbid thought — then a bright, cheerful thought.

4. Spend some time discussing special language that Poe used in the story. There are words such as

"phantasmagoric," "opium eaters," and "morbid acuteness." Let the students construct their own words for special effects. (For example, a grouchy old slob could be a grossgrump). Have a contest to see who can come up with the most new words. (Obscenities don't count.) In such a way you could discuss some of Poe's techniques used in writing the story. (Personification, onomatopoeia, alliteration).

5. For a dramatic exit the teacher could arrange for a speaker to talk on the subject of mental illness. Special mention could be made of an illness which manifests symptoms such as Roderick's. The area of depression and its symptoms could be discussed, especially as it pertains to students or adolescents.

Interpretive Inquiry

1. Poe has titled his story, "The Fall of the House of Usher." Is he talking about more than just the falling down of a structure? If so, what is he referring to?

2. Poe relies on special literary techniques such as imagery, alliteration, and symbolism to bring his story to life. An example would be "...an iciness, a sinking, a sickening of the heart." What does the "s" sound in that description do to change the mood or create a mood or emphasize a feeling in the reader? Does he mean to make you cold? Sick?

3. When the narrator sees the house, he remarks upon the vacant, eye-like windows and the few, white trunks of decayed trees. What picture does this conjure up in your mind? Is the House watching the nar-

rator? Can you see a face spring into your mind's eye? What would the tree trunks represent in this face?

4. The narrator, after inspecting the surroundings of the House, says there are certain combinations of very simple, natural objects which have the power to affect people in an unnatural and morbid way. What does he mean by this statement? What insight does this give you into the character of the narrator? Is he a rational and reasonable person, or an overimaginative and superstitious character? Why would Poe want us to believe the narrator as rational? Maybe he wants us to see him as superstitious. Why?

5. When the narrator describes the Usher family, he states they have been noted for their "peculiar sensibility of temperament." What does he mean by this phrase? He likewise says that the Usher family has put forth no enduring branches. What condition could have caused this? Is he referring to a physical, genetic flaw or a mental condition or both? What light does this throw on the nature of the Family Usher? Bad blood? Maybe cursed?

6. Roderick possessed a cadaverous complexion, thin pallid lips and a ghostly pallor of skin. What condition or disease could have caused this? Was he suffering from lack of sunshine, food, or perhaps tuberculosis? Does Poe want us to believe Roderick's symptoms are mental or physical? When the narrator describes the House, he mentions the tarn, the vacant, eye-like windows, and the fine

tangles of web-work across the eaves. Could he be describing something other than the house? What or whom?

7. What is a tarn? What color would it be? What word do we have in our vocabulary that is similar to tarn? (tar) Does the word tarn present a better image that river? What kind of image? Is that why Poe used it?

8. What causes the pestilent and mystic vapor that arises from the tarn? Could it be fog? Does the narrator see more to it than fog? Why?

9. The narrator detects a fissure in the House's walls. Could this fissure indicate something in Usher's personality? Mental?

10. When the narrator describes Usher's chamber, he sees rooms, large and lofty, and long, narrow windows allowing feeble gleams of light to trickle in. The eye has to struggle to reach the remote angles and recesses of the room. Do you have any idea of what Poe could be describing other than Roderick's living quarters?

11. Usher's mannerisms are inconsistent. His voice varies rapidly and his actions are alternately vivacious and sullen. What could cause such behavior? What is the modern-day, medical term for the condition which causes such strange behavior? In slang, is Roderick "cracked"? How does the fissure relate to this condition?

12. Roderick lived years within the walls of the dreary mansion. Did this have any bearing on his strange temperament? How so?

13. Roderick says he fears "Fear." But he owns a

library of fearful works. Why? Is he trying to scare himself?

14. In what artistic ways does Usher display his fanatical mind? Why does Poe present these artistic diversions to the reader? What do they tell the reader?

15. Usher draws a picture of a tunnel. What does this represent? If he drew it before Madeline's burial, does that mean he intentionally buried Madeline alive?

16. Usher quickly buries Madeline after her death. One of the reasons given was that the "obtrusive and eager inquiries on the part of her medical men" required a quick interment. What do you think Poe meant by this? Body snatching? Or was Usher just making up reasons to bury Madeline quickly?

17. Poe poured a great deal of time and effort into descriptive passages with great regard to setting. What does this tell you about Poe's style of writing? What does he emphasize in the story? Is this a character study or something else? Does he have more fun penning the set or embellishing the characters?

18. Poe uses words such as "phantasmagoric" and phrases such as "sensations of stupor" or "dreams of opium eaters." Does he want us to believe we are dreaming? Does he want us to think the narrator is dreaming? Is the story a dream? Roderick's or the narrator's?

19. When the narrator is first focused upon, he admits he may be superstitous. By the end of the story he is fully hysterical. Did he catch Roderick's disease?

Could this story be a study of the contagion of fear?

20. Poe tells the reader the place of Madeline's interment used to be a storage area for gun powder. He also says it is lined with copper. Why would he mention these two items? Is the gun powder still there? Why copper, and not lead or brick?

21. How was it possible for Madeline, weak after her great struggle to get out of the coffin, to climb the stairs to Roderick's chamber? Would the strange storm have any connection with her super human energy? How did she get to the top? How did Frankenstein get his energy?

22. What caused the House to crumble finally at the story's end? Again, remember the description of the tunnel and the storm. Was there an explosion? Does Poe tell us?

23. When the House falls, the narrator says it sounds like the voice of a thousand waters. What does this mean? What is the sound?

Intellectual Inquiry

1. Roderick says his sister's death would leave him the last of the ancient race of Usher. Would this be a frightening situation? Are any of you (students) the only child of an only child?

2. Do you think Roderick loved his sister or hated her for dying first? Is this why he buried her alive and then tried to scare himself to death? Do you know of anyone who is the last surviving member of a family? Does he or she behave differently because of this circumstance?

3. The narrator has admitted that he may be superstitious. Are you? Do things that are natural take on strange appearances at different times? When? Does the night or morning have any effect on this notion? Is it just the lighting that makes a difference or one's state of mind (alert vs. drowsy or tired)?

4. Poe refers to the mind as a chamber of remote angles and recesses. Do you picture the mind in the same way? Does your mind contain secret rooms or inaccessible places?

5. Poe describes the House, but the description applies to Roderick also. Is this consistent with life? Some people say dog owners look like their dogs. Do some people look like their houses?

6. (Tread carefully). The narrator speaks of Usher and his dream-like states. More than once he refers to after-dreams of opium eaters. Have you ever been detached from reality this way? On drugs? Day dreams? High from sports?

7. Usher can't stand certain fabrics, food, or sounds. Is this because he is mad or could it be a physical disorder? Can you think of a disease which could cause these symptoms? (Allergies?) Do you know of any one who has felt this way? Have you?

8. Roderick shares sensations with his sister, both when she is alive and as she is struggling within the coffin. Is this possible? Can twins share this type of telepathy? How about ordinary siblings?

9. "The Fall" is acclaimed as a story dealing with the contagion of fear. You have probably been a victim

of contagious laughter. Is fear contagious? Have you ever become fearful because someone else was afraid?

10. Usher was a product of the gloomy house he lived in so long. Could this happen? Are people's moods susceptible to their surroundings? Do colors play a part in this? How about sunlight? What makes you feel gloomy?

11. Roderick has been portrayed as a schizophrenic. What does this mean to you? Have you ever met someone whose moods alternate from high to low rapidly? Do you know of anyone who has had a nervous breakdown? Do your moods change rapidly at times?

12. Poe speaks of the tarn swallowing up the mansion in a voice of a thousand waters. Where could you go today to hear "a thousand waters"? (A waterfall, the ocean?)

The Minister's Black Veil

—Nathaniel Hawthorne

Improvisations

1. The day before taking up this story, the teacher might stand on a box or chair while conducting the class. After a period of time, observing the effects, the teacher could resume the normal teaching position and invite reactions from students. Ask the students what the major effect was. Were you a more imposing figure? Was your lecture/discussion

more overpowering? Was the pose unsettling? What?

2. On the day the story is discussed, have someone (another teacher, a student not a member of the class) sit through the class period wearing sunglasses. Have this person sit in a conspicuous place and ask him/her to observe the class. Near the end of the discussion the mystery person should leave quietly. If the students wish to discuss this incident (and they will), invite their reactions. Let them observe how many Goodman Gray's or Elizabeth's or other townspeople are in their midst.

3. Ask three of the students to prepare a class skit in which they are Mr. Hooper's next door neighbors. As a family, they are attempting to reach a decision about whether to move because of the strangeness of Mr. Hooper and his wearing of the black veil. One student takes the position that Hooper is an agent of the devil and thus feels impelled to move; another student takes the position that Hooper is an agent of God and thus doesn't want to move; the third student takes the position that Hooper is a tortured, unhappy person and is indifferent about whether or not to move. After the scenario, invite class reactions to and questions of the three students. Then let the class vote as to which solution is best.

4. Mr. Hooper became a very lonely man. Think of all the words you associate with loneliness (either a class project or an individual project). Then, write a poem or story in which you attempt to use all of the words you have associated with "loneliness." (Might be a

71

good creative exit from the story.)

Interpretive Inquiry

1. Hawthorne subtitles his story "A Parable." What is a parable? Why do you think Hawthorne refers to this story as a parable?

2. Mr. Hooper chose to wear a black veil. Why did he choose black? Do you think people might have reacted differently if the veil were another color? If so, what would some possible reactions be? When does someone usually wear a black veil?

3. Many of the people are frightened by the fact that Mr. Hooper wears the black veil. However, others seem somewhat amused by it, and some say he must have gone mad. What are some people afraid of? Do you think the black veil is a symbol of something awful? If so, what? Has Hooper gone mad?

4. Hawthorne does not tell us specifically why Mr. Hooper wears the black veil. Why are we left in the dark? Can you suggest some reasons why Mr. Hooper wears the veil? And why does he feel compelled to sleep with it on and to die with it on? He says it is "a type and a symbol." What does the veil symbolize? What could Mr. Hooper possibly have seen to make him want to wear the veil?

5. Mr. Hooper is a dismal figure in the community because "he has changed himself into something awful, only by hiding his face." Does this bother him in any way? Is he a happy person? Why or why not?

6. Elizabeth is the only character who is brave enough

to confront Mr. Hooper about the black veil. Does this mean that she is a strong character? If so, what makes her strong? Is she more rational or less rational than Mr. Hooper? How do you feel about her attempts? Should she have continued to try to talk to him? Why does she come back to nurse him on his death bed?

7. The story say, "Among all its bad influences, the black veil had one desirable effect, of making its wearer a very efficient clergyman." How could this be? What made him efficient for the congregation of his church? Did his sermons have some special message that was conveyed through his words?

8. Does Mr. Hooper seem like a stable person? Did he commit some terrible sin? According to the story, he says, "I look around me, and lo! on every visage a Black Veil!"

9. Mr. Hooper wore the veil until he died (and was buried with it on). Do you think his decision was a wise or foolish one? Did he accomplish anything by it?

10. Who was the girl that dies at the beginning of the story? Where is she mentioned again? Why is this girl important to the story or is she important? Did her death change Mr. Hooper? What happens of significance at her funeral? Do you think Mr. Hooper and the girl had a romantic attachment? A love affair?

11. Is Mr. Hooper an agent of God or the devil? Why do the church members begin to call him "Father" Hooper? Does he attain supernatural powers after he begins wearing the veil?

12. How does Death fit into the story? Is it one of the characters? Is it a powerful force?
13. Hawthorne in many of his stories is obsessed with the idea of unpardonable sins. Does this story suggest that maybe Mr. Hooper has commited an unpardonable sin? If so, what might it be? Is there such a sin in the eyes of God?

Intellectual Inquiry

1. People often react to colors differently. Can you think of some "good" and "bad" colors in our society? Do you dislike certain colors? Do any colors remind you of terrible things?
2. Mr. Hooper separates himself from others and never reveals his secret. Does everyone have secrets? Should secrets be revealed? Why do people keep secrets from one another? Is this harmful? Is it ever helpful? Is a secret ever worth separating yourself from everyone?
3. The veil that Mr. Hooper wears is a symbol. We have many symbols in our own society such as the flag, the cross, the dove, the hawk, and so on. Can you think of some other important symbols that are relevant to us today? Do symbols mean the same thing for each individual?
4. Hooper seems to suffer a great deal because of the black veil, yet he continues to wear it. Can you think of other people who continue to do something that causes them pain or problems? Is it ever beneficial in the long run?
5. Something as simple as a black veil alters Hooper greatly and causes a terrible reaction from his

friends. Appearance is very important in our society. Do you know of other examples of how changes in appearance can change attitudes of people? Did the black veil change Mr. Hooper's personality? Do changes in appearance ever affect personalities?

6. If Mr. Hooper lived in our society today, how would people react to him? What are some major differences between the people of our society and the people of his town? Are there some similarities also?

7. How do you feel about mistakes that you have made in your life? Is it best to live a life of gloom because of these mistakes or is there another alternative? Should people have to suffer for the rest of their lives for their mistakes? Should anyone ever have to be responsible for the mistakes of others?

8. If you were trying to hide something, who would it be hardest to hide it from? Who would know something was wrong whether you told them or not? Why?

9. Do people carry scars that no one else can see? If so, where might these scars be?

10. Have you ever felt alienated from people around you? How did it feel? What was its cause?

11. Have you ever felt you could see something in another person that others couldn't?

12. It has been said that the eyes are the mirror of the soul. What do you think of this statement?

13. If you looked at the world through a veil of darkness, what would that do to your mirror of the world?

Chapter 5

The Inquiry Method Applied: Novels

In this chapter again we have provided improvisational situations and ideas, along with interpretive and intellectual questions, for these five novels in this order:

With the possible exception of *The Chocolate War,* which is a 1970's publication (1974), we think you will agree we have included novels that have quite possibly been among the most popular (and again the most readily available) both with teachers and students since publication. Our Robert Cormier selection is a personal bias that we feel demands inclusion because of its widespread popularity and its subject matter and theme that speak so tellingly to young readers, particularly boys. Furthermore, we think Robert Cormier is one of the best, contemporary writers in America, writing almost exclusively for and about young people.

Lest you have not yet noticed, we should point out that *Lord of the Flies* is the only work included in this book that was not written by an American. We made the exception because of its universal popularity with teachers and young readers in this country, and, again, its subject matter and theme deal with young people (all boys, alas) in a period of isolation and alienation and the struggle between good and evil.

Of Mice and Men

— John Steinbeck

Improvisations

1. Improvise a skit. The characters needed are a father, a mother, a teenage boy, and several members of an irate community. Build the skit around this situation: The boy is told that the large dog that he raised from a pup has bitten several small children in the town. The dog will have to be destroyed. This is a rural community with no alternatives such as animal adoption shelters. How will the boy argue in behalf of the dog? How do the townspeople tell their side of the story? Which side of the argument do the parents take (a good, creative entry to the novel)?
2. Have several members of the class describe how they

feel about a favorite pet they have had for a long time — its faithfulness, its familiarity, the inconvenience it has caused at times.

3. Is it easier to learn what someone is really like by hearing a description of him or by listening to what he says? Test this by having someone describe an argument between two students. Then have the two students carry on that argument in front of the class. Which told you more about what kinds of people they were? Which method gave you more insight into their personalities? Point out to students that Steinbeck did an excellent job of using dialogue instead of description for these purposes in *Of Mice and Men.*

4. Role playing — Pick students to assume the roles of the farm hands. Have them improvise a skit in which these farm hands try to keep Curley from going after Lennie. How would they defend Lennie?

Interpretive Inquiry

1. What makes George and Lennie different and sets them apart from the other men on the farm? Why do you suppose they are the only characters in the novel who have last names? Why does Lennie want George to tell him so often the story of how they will someday "live off the fatta the lan' "?

2. What purpose is served by the difference in George's and Lennie's sizes? Which childlike characteristics are present in Lennie? Why is George a strong disciplinarian? Why is the boss suspicious about Lennie's refusal to speak for himself and to answer

the questions?

3. Why is George constantly ridiculing Lennie about the trouble and inconvenience he causes him? Why doesn't it hurt Lennie's feelings? How does George make amends for the criticism each time and cover his real feelings for Lennie?

4. What is "rollin' up a stake" and buying a place of their own a symbol of? What would the small farm mean to George? to Candy? to Crooks? to Lennie? Could it ever become a reality?

5. What parallel can be drawn between Candy and his old dog and George and Lennie? What is ironical about George being Lennie's executioner? Why is George's shooting of Lennie an act of great compassion? What is George's real motive in asking Candy to let him return to the bunkhouse before calling attention to the dead body?

6. Why does Curley become frenzied enough to attack Lennie? Did Curley pick on Lennie because he was dull-witted or because he was so big?

7. How do Curley and his wife serve as the point upon which the final destruction of Lennie hinges? How does Steinbeck weave them into the story to prepare us for this?

8. Who emerges as the loneliest character in the novel? Is there any hint of a potential friendship for Candy? for Crooks? Why would Curley's wife, who had proved that she could be attractive to men and who could have been in the movies, reach out for contact with this huge, hulking, dull-witted man?

9. Curley's wife is made to be painfully aware of her

loneliness and isolation when Candy and Crooks try to force her to leave the harness room. Instead, she uses her position to strike out and put them "in their places." Is it possible to view her as a mean person? What is so pathetic about a person of lofty dreams who must settle for such lowly company and conversation?

10. What connotation does being a ranch hand carry with it? What kind of isolation is suggested by a room with unpainted floors, empty beds with only their burlap ticking showing, and apple boxes nailed to the wall for shelving? How does Steinbeck use this setting and these kinds of workers to set up a contrast for George and Lennie? Why not have them work in a factory or on a loading dock, for instance?

11. Were the farmhands tolerant of Lennie? Do you think they were kind to him? Would things have been different if George weren't along? Were they willing to forgive Lennie when they realized that he had committed murder?

12. What social distinction does race impose even among the lower class of farm laborers? Is Crooks satisfied to stay "in his place"? How do you know? Why is he so edgy about having the white men come into his quarters in the harness room? Is it this isolation or his painfully crippled body which evokes our sympathy for Crooks? Who is the one person who does not make a distinction, does not even notice Crooks' blackness? Why?

13. What kind of imagery is dominant throughout the

story? What animal is Lennie himself compared to in the early scene by the stream? How does this animal imagery fit in with the theme of loneliness? Do animals experience loneliness? Do they have any advantages over man?

14. Is the language of the novel appropriate to the characters? Why does saying the dog "slang her pups" last night and calling Curley's wife "jail bait all set on a trigger" give the story flavor? How much does this ranch hand dialect add to the atmosphere and characterization of the novel?

15. Why do you think Steinbeck used dialogue to develop his characters and circumstances and kept descriptive passages to a minimum? What can dialogue do for characterization that description can't?

16. What does the pastoral setting of the opening and closing scenes mean to the plot of the story? What do the bunkhouse and barn represent? What do these settings mean to the characters? Which means safety and friendship? Which means interaction and danger? Why is it ironic that George made sure Lennie would return to the bushes by the stream if there were ever any trouble?

Intellectual Inquiry

1. Is a human being capable of living without hope for a brighter future, something better to come? Is it possible for human beings to live without comradeship?

2. How do you personally feel about spending time

alone? Could you live alone? Would you like working at a solitary occupation? What kind of personality is necessary for a person to be a "loner"? What is meant by the expression "being lonely in a crowd"? Have you ever been lonely in a crowd of people? Did you know why or why not?

3. How do you explain to a small child why he cannot hold (or pet too hard) a newborn puppy or kitten? Why does a child like to have the same stories read or told to him over and over?

4. Are there any circumstances under which murder is or should be forgivable? How do you feel about capital punishment? In which instances, if any, is it justified?

5. What do you feel should be the law's attitude about retarded people who commit crimes? Is a person guilty if he can't remember having committed the crime?

6. How does the average "man on the street" react to a person who is mentally deficient? Is physical deficiency equally as or even more pitiable? How does our treatment of the mentally retarded differ from around 1937 when Steinbeck wrote *Of Mice and Men*?

7. In this novel, Steinbeck was obviously concerned with exploring the meaning of loneliness. Which do you think is the most pathetic — the loneliness of being different, the loneliness of being without love, the loneliness of feeling old and useless, or the loneliness of being unable to reach out and have a relationship with someone?

The Old Man and the Sea

— Ernest Hemingway

Improvisations

1. Role playing

   Santiago's fishing excursions had been unsuccesful for eighty-four days, and "many of the fishermen made fun of the old man and he was not angry. Others . . . looked at him and were sad. But they did not show it." The following role-playing situation might help students better appreciate how difficult humility and control of temper are in the face of peer disapproval. They also might be made more aware of the type of person Santiago was and may enter the story with a better developed understanding of and sympathy for the main character. Have different students assume the following roles while the remainder of the class is divided into two groups: one that makes fun of the student and another that is sympathetic to the student. Roles:

   > an unsuccessful football player
   > an unsuccessful drama student
   > an unsuccessful cheerleader

2. The dramatic situation below might better prepare the students for imaginative entry into the work:

   a. Setting: a deserted football field
      Character: one football player
      Action: the character must bring himself to practice game plays all by himself until he is physically exhausted

2. The dramatic situation below might better prepare the students for imaginative entry into the work:
   a. Setting: a deserted football field
      Character: one football player
      Action: the character must bring himself to practice game plays all by himself until he is physically exhausted
   b. The primary questions posed to the student actor and to the audience might be: "Why should I work myself to physical exhaustion when I can get by with less effort? There isn't even one person around to witness how thorough and conscientious I am. What's the point in working this hard?"
3. Possible scene one might use that suggests a creative means for involving the students in the experience of the work is the last scene, wherein Santiago awakens from his sleep and converses with Manolin.
   a. Two students might first dramatize the dialogue to refresh the scene in the minds of the class.
   b. Then, as a "lesson" in sensitivity and effective one-to-one communication, two students, using their own dialogue, would enact a similar scene: one student has just suffered a defeat and the other student, his friend, speaks with him after the incident.
   c. The questions that might occur to the students, or that could be directed to them, would be of the following nature: How does one comfort a friend who has suffered a loss of some kind? How does one effectively communicate the feeling that he cares without making the other

person lose his dignity and feel inferior? How might one communicate understanding and sympathy without pity?

Interpretive Inquiry

1. In the first paragraph Hemingway directly states how unlucky the old man is. In the second he describes how old Santiago is. What effect does such a direct approach to the main character create so early in the story? Hemingway tells us that the old man's sail "furled . . . looked like the flag of permanent defeat," yet the old man's eyes were "undefeated." What clue does this seemingly irreconcilable contrast give us to Santiago's character? Why is it significant that Santiago's eyes were "the same color as the sea"? The old man was "salao, which is the worst form of unlucky," but Santiago says he would rather "be exact" than lucky. What does he mean by that?

2. Santiago has "attained humility," and he feels humility is not disgraceful, nor does it carry with it a loss of true pride. How are humility and pride parts of Santiago? How can both exist in the same person?

3. What are some of Santiago's virtues? How are they demonstrated in the story? As virtuous as Santiago is, does he have any faults? Despite his physical pain, Santiago never gives up. Is his perseverance realistic? Is he a believable character?

4. How long does the battle between Santiago and the fish last? Considering the age of the old man, is the length of the battle realistic? Is the outcome

realistic? What does Santiago have going for him that might make up for his age?

5. How would you describe the relationship between Santiago and Manolin? How has the relationship betweeen them developed? How does Manolin keep Santiago "alive"? Why does Santiago wish Manolin were along when he fights with the marlin?

6. Why would there be interest in American baseball teams in Cuba? What parallels does Santiago find between himself and Joe DiMaggio? What draws him to the baseball player? Why does he feel he must be "worthy of the great DiMaggio" during his battle with the marlin?

7. When an object is given human characteristics, it is "personified." How does Santiago personify his left hand? Why does he talk to it and "eat" for it? In recalling the episode of the hand game he played with the Negro when he was young, Santiago says that he had tried practice matches with his left hand but the hand had been a "traitor and would not do what he called on it to do and he did not trust it." How is Santiago's left hand traitorous in his battle with the fish? Does his left hand bring him bad luck?

8. In another personification, Santiago thinks of the sea as a woman. What womanly characteristics does he attribute to *la mar*? Why do other fishermen call the sea by the masculine form, *el mar*?

9. Santiago regards the fish as his brother, yet he kills it anyway. Why does he question his right to kill the marlin? What is the outcome of his questioning? Is he satisfied with not understanding if he is right or if

he is instead guilty of the sin of pride?

10. Santiago says that fishermen talk little to one another when they are in the boats. Santiago, however, talks a great deal to himself. Why? What is the difference between the thoughts he says aloud and those he will only think but not give voice to?

11. Why does Santiago say to the marlin, "Come on and kill me. I do not care who kills who"? He asks himself, "is he bringing me in or am I bringing him in?" How does Santiago feel he was able to kill the fish? What was his only superiority over the marlin that enabled him to kill it? The marlin is worthy of Santiago's admiration but not all creatures in the sea are. Why does he love the sea turtles, whom he calls "stupid loggerheads," yet hate the beautiful Portugese man-of-war? He respects the Mako shark, the *dentuso,* who is the first to tear at his marlin, but he hates shovel-nosed sharks, the *galanos.* Why? What difference does Santiago see in the two kinds of sharks?

12. Santiago says, ". . . man is not made for defeat. . . . A man can be destroyed but not defeated." How is this a controlling idea (theme) in the story? Was Santiago destroyed? Why or why not? Why does Santiago refuse to believe he was beaten when he returns to shore with only the head of the marlin?

13. One of Santiago's recurring dreams is that about the lions he saw on the beach in Africa. Why does Santiago dream about the lions? Why is it significant that in the boat he finally dreams of them? What do they mean, or symbolize, in the story?

14. At the end of the story a tourist mistakes the backbone of the great fish for that of a shark. What is ironic about her mistake? What might have been Hemingway's point in using the irony? Why do you think he chose, however, not to end the novella with the ironic tone, but with the old man's dream of the lions?

15. It is seemingly impossible to paraphrase a poem and still convey what the poet was saying and how he was saying it. Try paraphrasing the following paragraph from *The Old Man and the Sea*:

> He took all of his pain and
> what was left of his strength
> and his long gone pride and he
> put it against the fish's agony
> and the fish came over onto his
> side and swam gently on his
> side, his bill almost touching
> the planking of the skiff and
> started to pass the boat, long,
> deep, wide, silver and barred
> with purple and interminable in
> the water.

What is lost in paraphrasing this paragraph: What stands out about the language? How is the prose of this paragraph, and of the rest of the novella, for that matter, in some ways like poetry?

Intellectual Inquiry

1. Santiago had both personal reasons and practical reasons for catching the fish. Which reasons do you

think were more important to him? When you face a challenging situation, do you work harder if the end is to gain practical rewards or if the end brings personal satisfaction? Why?

2. Despite his physical pain, Santiago never gave up. Why? Does so much perseverance seem reasonable/realistic to you? Do you think it would have made better sense for him to have given up the fight? Where along the way might you have been tempted to give up?

3. There are several times during Santiago's struggle with the fish when he wished Manolin were there. Would the boy's presence have made Santiago handle the situation (or act) in a different way? In your own experience, what effect does (or might) the presence of a friend or an audience have on one's actions?

4. Santiago states, "I believe it is a sin [not to hope]." How important is hope in the story? Is there a place for hope in our everyday lives and activities? What part does it play?

5. Why did the old man want to see the fish that he had hooked but that had not yet surfaced? Why do you think it was so important for him to know what he was fighting? Compare Santiago's situation to that of a person whose doctor sends him for tests because something is wrong, but the doctor cannot be sure what the problem is. Do you think that if the person later found out he had cancer, he would feel a sense of relief knowing what disease he was fighting? Why or why not?

6. Why does Santiago decide to say ten Our Fathers and ten Hail Marys although he admits he is not religious? Why does he promise to make a religious pilgrimage if he catches the fish? Do you think he really will make the pilgrimage? In the midst of battling the marlin he says, "I'll say a hundred Our Fathers and a hundred Hail Marys. But I cannot say them now. Consider them said, he thought." Why does he say this? What do you think is Santiago's view of religion? Is he superstitious? Do we ever make promises to God or to other people — parents, say — in desperate situations and then not keep them later? Why do we do this sometimes?

7. Santiago and Manolin were apparently very close to one another. In reference to the "pot of yellow rice and fish," both knew it did not exist, though neither of them openly admitted it. Was this dishonest? Did it harm anybody? Did it benefit anybody? Have you ever refrained from openly questioning a friend's statement that both of you know is not true? Why?

8. How did Manolin react to Santiago's "defeat"? Did he try to comfort Santiago? If you had suffered a defeat as Santiago had, would you have wanted pity from a friend? Why?

To Kill a Mockingbird

— Harper Lee

Improvisations

1. Before students read the novel, have them relate

at least one of their own childhood experiences and how it affected them at that particular time in their lives. This could be done orally or it could be a written exercise.

2. Set up a classroom court scene, but reverse the circumstances of the trial, having a white man attacking a black girl and being judged by an all-black jury. Student creations here should lead to some very interesting insights and implications.

3. Student actors could role play the part of a person being discriminated against. Students might investigate a situation in which a group of young people are making fun of a person who is standing apart from the group.

4. Student actors could be assigned parts as members of the jury. Other students could ask them questions as to why they voted as they did.

Interpretive Inquiry

1. Who is the narrator of the story? Approximately how old is she when she relates this tale? How is her language like that of a child? Does she ever exaggerate? In which particular situations? How does writing from a child's point of view make the story more flavorful? Does it reduce its believability? Do you consider this account of the story to be an accurate one? How do you think the story would be changed if it were written by a long-time resident of Maycomb County?

2. Define "prejudice" in your own words. What effect does a person's prejudice have on the way he views

life? How did prejudice against Negroes develop in the South? What does the term "poor white trash" mean? What kind of lifestyle did such people have? How were *they* (poor white trash) discriminated against? Would the trial scene have been more dramatic if Tom Robinson were accused of attacking a middle-class white girl? Why did the author choose to have a person like Mayella Ewell as a leading character?

3. At the opening of the story we read that "Being Southerners, it was a source of shame to some members of the family that we had no recorded ancestors on either side of the Battle of Hastings." Why do some people place great value on ancestry? How can it ruin you? How did Aunt Alexandra view the idea of her background? In what ways did she try to mold the Finch children into her ideal pattern?

4. What is Atticus's definition of compromise? Give at least two examples from the story in which people made compromises. How can compromise be an instrument for evil?

5. Explain what Atticus means when he tells Scout she must "climb into a person's skin and walk around in it." How does Atticus make Jem and Scout aware of the burdens of other people?

6. Why did Mr. Radley cement the tree where presents were left for the children? What did the tree represent?

7. How do Jem and Scout address their father? *Why* do you think they call him by his first name? At the outset of the story Scout remarks, "Jem and I found

our father satisfactory: he played with us, read to us, and treated us with courteous detachement." What does the word detachment mean? Is this a fair evaluation, in your opinion, of the man, or is it a "childish" evaluation? Does your concept of Atticus change as the plot develops? How?

8. In what year did the events of the story take place? Where did the story take place? Describe in your own words the town of Maycomb as seen through Scout's eyes. Why do you think that Harper Lee chose this sleepy setting? Would the tale be more effective set in a big, bustling town? Why or why not? How would the author's treatment of Boo be altered?

9. What was the significance of Judge Taylor selecting Atticus to defend Tom Robinson? How was the long deliberation of the jury significant to the story? Were you surprised at the jury's decision? How did the author help build tension at the trial scene?

10. How is Dill's upbringing different from that of the Finch children? It was said of Dill that he prefers "his own twilight world." What is a twilight world like?

11. Who is Boo Radley, according to rumor? What is the real Boo Radley like? Why did Boo lock himself into the house? How is the title of the book related to this man?

12. Why does Atticus tell the children it is a sin to kill a mockingbird?

13. What is Atticus trying to tell the children when he says he wants them "to see what real courage is, in-

stead of getting the idea that courage is a man with a gun in his hand"? Who do you see in the story you would classify as being a courageous person?

14. Has the author succeeded in presenting Tom as a strong character? Was Tom a symbol for the Negro people?

15. What is Scout trying to tell Atticus when she tells him it would be like killing a mockingbird if Boo Radley were brought to trial?

16. While waiting for the jury's decision, Scout described her father's fight for Robinson's life: "It was like watching Atticus walk into the street, raise a rifle to his shoulder and pull the trigger, but watching all the time knowing the gun was empty." Did Atticus have enough evidence (ammunition) to win the case? Did Atticus actually lose the case? Was Tom Robinson proved sufficiently guilty? If Atticus hadn't been appointed to take the case, would he have defended Tom anyway? If Atticus knew he had only a slight chance of winning, why did he risk his life and reputation to protect Tom as he did?

Intellectual Inquiry

1. How might Atticus be called a "modern hero"? Do you think he is a hero? Why/why not? What "heroic" characteristics does he have? Why was it so important to Jem that his father be a good shot and also athletic? How does our society determine what a real *man* is? How is this concept of a man related to the American dream of success and power? How does the sports world contribute to the

idea of the all-American male?

2. Do you believe that Atticus should have revealed Boo Radley as the man who killed Mr. Ewell? Why/why not? Didn't this involve deceitfulness or giving a false impression? Is it ever right to withold the truth to protect another human being? Does the phrase "What you don't know won't hurt you" really make sense? Must the telling of the truth rely on circumstances?

3. Name as many instances as you can recall in the book which involve the act of reading. The children read to whom? What effect did this have on the Finch children — on Mrs. Dubose? How was Scout affected when her father read to her? What do you think is so special about having a person read to you? Why do parents often read stories aloud to their children (other than the fact that the children are unable to read themselves)?

4. Would you like to live in the town of Maycomb? Why/why not? What are some of the advantages/disadvantages of small town life? Why is there such a popular movement in our country to get back to the country style of living? Is it possible to "go back" to those good ol' days and still be happy? Can the giving up of luxuries purge us and bring back all that wholesomeness we long for?

5. Scout is recalling many childhood experiences in this book. Do they seem realistic to you? Can you recall any person who in your childhood years seemed very scary? Have you ever returned to a place where you had spent many hours as a child (i.e. a treehouse,

playhouse) and found that it had changed? What had actually happened? Do you think you have the same capacity to imagine *now* as you did then? Why do we cease to play childhood games?

6. Would you want a father like Atticus? Do you agree with his approach to parenthood?

7. Do you think a person's most valuable education comes from the experiences she/he encounters in life? Is it possible for schools to prepare people to cope with the problems and frustrations they will encounter in the world?

8. What is meant by "man's inhumanity to man"? Do you think Harper Lee was trying to make the reader feel that the people of Maycomb were being inhumane to Tom and Boo? If so, who are Tom's and Boo's in your society? in this state? in this country?

9. How do you define bravery? Does your definition fit Atticus' when he calls Mrs. Dubose the bravest person he had ever known?

10. How do you define justice? Do you think the courts today uphold justice according to your definition? What might have happened to Tom if his trial had taken place in Southern California instead of the Deep South?

Lord of the Flies

-William Golding

Improvisations

1. Before reading the novel, select three boys to

prepare a short scenario for class presentation dealing with the following situation: a group of boys are on a mountain hike with an adult guide. All become lost. The guide leaves to seek help, instructing the boys to stay put until he returns. There are three natural leaders in the group of boys - one, who is quite intelligent and receives high grades in school, but is rather small physically and not athletic; another who is big, quite athletic, popular, but a bit of a goof off; the third, a big, rugged boy who is intimidating to others because he has a reputation as a bully. Improvise a situation among the three as they contend for leadership of the group. After the presentation, have the class decide who should be the leader. Majority rules.

2. Before reading the story, ask one or two of the class artists to sketch on the chalkboard (or on paper for later referral) their perception of a "lord of the flies." Let class members make suggestions to the artist(s). Then, after reading the novel, ask the artists to sketch the "Lord of the Flies" as Golding depicts him. Class can make suggestions. Compare.

3. Ask students to bring in pictures from newspapers or magazines of people who they feel look like leaders or people they would choose as leaders. Along with these pictures ask them to bring in pictures of actual leaders in society (past and/or present). Ask students to discuss the intellectual, physical, and personal qualities they perceive in the pictures they selected as compared to the pictures of actual leaders. What commonalities appear to be present?

What differences? Where do Ralph and Jack fit into these commonalities or differences?

4. Select two good, willing students (might be a good idea while reading the novel) to make the following pitches to the class: One student tells the class that she/he is forming a study group to prepare for upcoming examinations in the class (and other classes for that matter). The other student wants to plan a class party (Christmas, Thanksgiving, you name it) and wants volunteers to assist her/him. Allow the groups to form for a few minutes to work out preliminary plans. Then, discuss with students why they joined the particular group they are in. This, then, may be a good time to discuss why certain boys joined Ralph's group and others Jack's group (Sneaky, but fun).

Interpretive Inquiry

1. Why does Ralph feel order and basic rules must be maintained even though the boys are free on an isolated island with no adults? Why is he chosen as chief?
2. Why is the Conch shell important? Why does Jack disregard its importance?
3. What is significant about Jack's leading the choir boys in strict military formation?
4. What is Jack's method of leadership? Historically or presently, can you think of any leaders like Jack?
5. Jack fails in his first attempt to kill a pig and consequently makes excuses for this failure. Why does he make these excuses? Can one get more of an idea of

Jack's personality through his excuses?

6. What is the significance of Ralph's exhilaration when he becomes involved in attacking a pig with the other boys?

7. Who or what is the "lord of the flies"? What is its importance in this story? The boar's head says, "Fancy thinking the Beast was something you could hunt and kill." What does this mean?

8. What is the significance of the boys' reenacting the pig hunt by using another boy as the pig?

9. Why is Piggy so concerned with learning everyone's names? Does this fact lend insight into his personality?

10. Why do the boys constantly mock Piggy and not take him seriously? Do you sympathize with Piggy? Why/why not?

11. Simon often wanders off into the jungle by himself and communes with nature. He also helps the young boys gather fruit, and he participates in building the shelters. How would you generalize Simon's personality by his activities? Do his actions and personality remind you of any historical figures?

12. How did you feel when Simon was killed? Why does Piggy pretend he had nothing to do with Simon's death? How do you feel when Piggy dies?

13. Which of the boys consider the signal fires and shelters important? Which care more about hunting? What does this tell us about each group of boys?

14. Why do the boys desert Ralph and join Jack? What does your answer tell you about the kind of society

they have on the island?

15. What does "allegory" mean? Allegorically, what do you think Ralph stands for? Piggy? Jack? Simon?
16. Why are the boys afraid of the dead parachutist? How does Simon react to the parachutist?
17. Who are the "Littl'uns"? How do they generally act?
18. If Ralph's age were not told in the story, how old would you think he was? Why did you decide on this age?
19. Is the language used by the boys believable? Do boys age fourteen and younger talk the way these boys do?
20. The boys are not from America. What country are they from? How can you tell this from their language?
21. How is the language different when Simon is talking or thinking from when Ralph and Jack are fighting? How does the author use language to tell us about a character's personality?
22. Whenever the conch is blown, what do the others do? When it is held by one person while they speak, what do the others do? What can we say the conch stands for or symbolizes? What does the killing of the boar symbolize? Does Ralph's grief over the "end of innocence" relate to this symbolism?
23. When a statement is made and the opposite occurs, it is ironic. An author can also show irony by allowing the unexpected to happen. What statements and incidents did you find ironic in the story?
24. Are the characters in the story believable? If they

weren't in this period of isolation, do you think they would still have the same personalities?

25. Piggy is probably the deepest thinker of the group. Why do you suppose no one listens to him?

26. How is Jack's act of giving part of the kill to the beast based on fear? Does this action suggest a reverting to primitive society?

27. When the boys return to their normal society, do you think Ralph and Jack will ever become friends? Will they be different people or will they return to their normal, pre-island ways?

28. Why did Golding use all male characters? Do you think the story might have been different if all the characters had been female? Why? Why not?

29. Why is it ironic that the fire started by the hunters in the effort to kill Ralph attracts the naval cruise?

30. Some would argue that this story is full of Christian symbolism with Simon as the Christ figure. What incidents, actions, and words seemingly support this notion?

Intellectual Inquiry

1. Ralph complains that the boys enjoy discussions at meetings and are enthusiastic about new ideas - but only for a short time; after a few minutes they lose interest in any constructive activity and wander away to play, eat, or sleep. Have you ever been involved in a common cause group? What are the attitudes of the members during the meeting? Shortly after? A few days later?

2. If Ralph were an adult, do you think the boys would

listen and follow rules better? Do you accept the authority of an adult over a peer? Why/why not? Are there some adults that you respect more than others? Why/why not?

3. The boys become accustomed to the weather and the passage of the sun during the day. Every morning the sun rises and the air is fresh and clear. At noon the sun is high and its heat and light are unbearable. In the late afternoon it grows cool again, and it is soon dark. How does Golding use the image of the rhythm of the day to describe the attitudes and personalities of the boys? Do you think they were affected by these rhythms because they were stranded and isolated on a deserted island or are human beings naturally affected by weather, temperature, sun, and darkness? Are you affected by the rhythms of the day?

4. One night, Jack tried to persuade Ralph to go up the mountain. Did Ralph eventually go or did he stay back? What was his reason for doing what he did? Have you ever been in the situation where you would be called a "coward" or "chicken" if you did not do something? Did you go through with it or stay back? What were your reasons for doing so?

5. The boys were fearful of "beasts" on the island. Do you think they just imagined these beasts? When you were young, did you see "beasts" in the dark? Did you think they were real? What did you do when you saw these "beasts"?

6. Simon often when to his shelter in the jungle to relax and commune with nature. Do you have a hideaway

where you can be by yourself? Besides to be alone, for what other reasons do you go to this place?

7. Why do the boys respond so readily to the sound of the conch shell being blown? Are there certain sounds that you respond to automatically? At school, what are sounds that students react to?

8. The boys acted differently with their painted faces and long hair. Do you act differently when you are dressed in costume at a masquerade or Halloween party? Why/why not? How do you act and feel when you are hidden behind a mask or make-up?

9. Jack constantly bullies Piggy. Do you know of a person who is constantly picking on someone? Why do people pick on other people or one particular person? Do you know of a person who is constantly made fun of? How do you think this person feels?

10. Have you ever had to choose between doing what you want to do and what you ought to do? How did you feel if you did what you wanted? How about if you did what you ought to do?

11. Do you act differently around adults than you do around teenagers? Why? Do you act differently when there are young children around?

12. Do you agree that people are never quite what we think they are? Is there a "beast" in all of us? Explain.

13. Is it inherent in mankind for one to want to feel power over another person or creature? Is violence (even the urge to kill) inherent in all of us?

14. By studying the different traits of the boys on the island, one might conclude that each boy is not a

separate individual but rather a small part of the make up of one human being. Pursue this idea.

15. If you had a chance to start a new society on an island, what provisions would you take? Would you take all we have now in modern conveniences? What rules and regulations would be necessary? How might you get all of the members to do their share in peace and harmony and still not alienate anyone?

The Chocolate War

— Robert Cormier

Improvisations

1. Three students wearing fashion jeans try to convince a student wearing old cords to change his (maybe her) style of dress — role playing, using a variety of arguments and counter arguments. This dramatic situation might lead to a discussion of fair and unfair means of persuasion.

2. The teacher gives the class a different assignment and then produces a box of marbles (or whatever) and tells the class that only the person who draws the black marble has to do the assignment. A variation on this activity could be: each student draws a marble; anyone drawing a white marble is excused from the assignment.

3. If Jerry died as a result of his injuries in the fight, who would be tried for murder? What would the evidence be? Who would be the witnesses? Role-play a court trial with different students assigned to act

out different parts.

4. Role-play a homecoming at Trinity School ten years after the events described in the novel. What would Jerry, Archie, Obie, Goober, Carter, Janza and Brother Leon be like? Who would not show up? Why?

5. Role-play a conversation between two students about Jerry's refusal to sell chocolates. Variations could be: before it was known that it was a Vigils' assignment; after Jerry's assignment was finished and he still refused to sell chocolates; before and after the Vigils started supporting the sale. (Public opinion about Jerry's actions is different at different times in the story.)

6. Write a letter to Trinity School from Jerry's father explaining why Jerry will not be returning for his sophomore year. Decide before you write the letter how much of the true story Jerry would have shared with his father.

Interpretive Inquiry

1. What is Jerry's motivation for defying the Vigils and Brother Leon? How do Jerry's feelings about the quality of his father's life influence his decision about selling the chocolates?

2. Why does Jerry stare at the Hippies on the Common? What are "Hippies"? Does Jerry envy them? Is he "middle-aged at fourteen"?

3. What new thing does Jerry learn about himself after the fight with Emile Janza?

4. What motivates Archie? Why does he always have to

be two steps ahead of everyone else?

5. Why does Obie admire Archie? Why does he hate Archie? What is the nature of their relationship?

6. How are Brother Leon and Archie alike? How are they different?

7. What is Brother Leon afraid of? What is Archie afraid of? What is Carter afraid of?

8. What motivates Emile Janza? Is Emile Janza really an "animal"? How does he feel about Archie and the Vigils?

9. What will "guys like Archie and Janza...do to the world once they leave Trinity"?

10. What does Goober feel during and after the destruction of Brother Eugene's room? What does this tell us about Goober's character? Why does he go through with the prank despite his feelings?

11. How does the "chocolate war" change Goober?

12. Do the other students do anything to support Jerry? What do they do? Why do they react to the situation this way?

13. What does Brian Cochran believe in? Given those beliefs, how well does he fit in with what is going on at Trinity School?

14. How does the "black box" provide control over the Assigner? How is Carter's influence like that of the "black box"?

15. What purpose do the religious references serve in *The Chocolate War*? Why are these references ironic in this particular setting?

16. Why do the Vigils get away with their cruel pranks? What do the Brothers want? How does the Brothers'

attitude allow the Vigils to exist? Are the Brothers "afraid to disturb the universe"? Why?

17. How is school spirit abused at Trinity?

18. How would the story be different if it took place at a girls' school? How would the story be different if it took place at a public school?

19. The novel begins and ends with "murder." How are these two events similar? How are they different?

20. How does Jerry's silence during Brother Leon's mistreatment of Gregory Bailey foreshadow the other students' unwillingness to defy the Vigils and to support Jerry? What other foreshadowings can you find?

21. What do the religious symbols in the novel mean? Why does Jerry compare himself to St. Peter? How are Obie and Archie different in their attitudes toward Jesus? Of what do the shadows of the goalposts remind Obie? Why is this symbol significant in terms of the theme of the novel? How does Brother Leon use religious references? Who is the "Unholy Trinity" at Trinity School? How are Crucifixion references and symbols used at the end of the novel?

22. What does Jerry mean when he tells the coach, "I'm playing ball"? What is the double meaning here?

23. What is ironic about the line on the first page of Chapter 1: "He had never felt so lonely in his life, abandoned, defenseless"?

24. Could both Brother Leon and Jerry have won the "chocolate war"?

Intellectual Inquiry

1. Have you ever taken a stand against a tradition or accepted practice? Did you ever defy the "in" crowd? What happened? How did you feel?
2. Have you ever accepted praise you didn't deserve? Why? How did it make you feel? (Jerry feels guilty when he is praised for being cool when he really feels terrified.)
3. Have you ever belonged to a gang or a secret club? Have you ever belonged to a powerful leadership group at school? Are such groups good or bad? Why?
4. Have you ever betrayed a friend? A cause? Yourself?
5. Do you think you are capable of violence? Under what circumstances might you be capable of violence?
6. Do you hate or enjoy confrontations? Why?
7. Jerry finds joy and release in football. Goober finds this in running. Brian finds it in driving his Chevy. Why are these tension breakers necessary? What do you do to relax and renew yourself?
8. What does making a commitment mean to you?
9. What are some of your schools's traditions? Are traditions good or bad? Why? Would you like to abolish certain traditions? Who starts traditions?
10. How would the story be different if it took place at your school?
11. What is school spirit? Is it important? Why?
12. Does a philosophy of "do your own thing" work? In what situations might it work, and in what situa-

tions would it probably fail? Is it a dangerous philosophy?

13. Who makes the rules in life? Who should make the rules?

14. How do you feel about the quality of your parents' lives? Do adults lead boring or exciting lives? Is your life more or less meaningful than that of your parents? Do you dread or look forward to growing up?

15. Are there any heroes in life? Is there anyone you can trust? Can you always trust yourself?

16. Are individuals important? Are they more or less important than a school or organization? Why?

17. What is conformity? Is it good or bad to conform? To what should or do we conform? Why do we conform? Why do we rebel?

18. Is the world really made of victims and victimizers? Of winners and losers? Are these labels permanent? What makes it possible for a person to be a survivor?

19. When is a joke or prank funny, and when is it cruel and sadistic?

20. Are teachers like everyone else? Are teachers above corruption? Should they be above corruption? Should they be better and purer than anyone else? Why or why not?

Chapter 6

The Inquiry Method Applied: Plays

In this chapter we have provided improvisational situations and ideas, as well as interpretive and intellectual questions, for these two plays:

1. Death of a Salesman
                              — Arthur Miller
                                    P. 108

2. The Glass Menagerie
                              — Tennessee Williams
                                    P. 114

Why only two plays, you may ask. It seems to us that in the literature curriculum in so many schools the reading and study of longer plays is often sacrificed to novels or any of the other genres. We have no quarrel with this fact, necessarily, but this explains why we have included only two works rather than our standard five. We might add further that the drama selections used with young readers are more often pap than protein, so we decided to use two blockbusters that demand inclusion in the literature curriculum because they are probably two of the best and most widely acclaimed American plays written in this century.

Finally, modern anthologies rarely include a rich selection of plays and they usually include very few, the limitations on space always being a problem. Be that as it may, if young readers are to read American drama, and they certainly should, then let's at least read those plays which represent the best Americans possess in the genre. *Death of a Salesman* and *The Glass Menagerie* (both widely available) fit this qualification, and they offer to young readers the kinds of characters and situations they can relate to because they are the characters and situations that speak with philosophical energy to the modern American experience of the common man.

Death of a Salesman

-Arthur Miller

Improvisations

1. Before reading the play, invite class discussion about an important experience which occurred when students were quite young (perhaps 8-10 years). Where did it happen? How did they feel? How did it affect them? How do they feel about it now? Knowing what they know now, how would they react to the same situation if it occurred today? The idea here is to lead students to the fact that people change. The activity could serve them well in puzzling out the Willy/Biff (father/son) relationship in the play.

2. Before reading the play, select two good students (actors) to dramatize a father/son relationship. Ask them to pick a topic and work out a brief scenario of an argument between father and son. Then pose various questions to the class about the dramatization. Was the argument realistic? Were father and son rational or were they emotional? Have you ever had this kind of experience at home with a parent or

family member? How do you react to family arguments? How do your parents react? How would you like them to react?

3. Have the class list various kinds of music they think would be appropriate for and would enhance each major character in the play.

4. In groups of four or five have students go through the play to find examples of Willy contradicting himself. This will help them discover how Willy is living in both a real and imaginary world where he sees things momentarily as they are and at almost the same time sees them as he would like them to be -conforming to his own illusions.

5. After discussing the play, assign certain students to play the parts of Linda, Biff, Hap, Charley, and Ben. Then have the rest of the class ask questions of these characters as to their views on Willy Loman's life and death.

6. Creative exit: Have each student write a brief account of what might have happened had Linda not persuaded Willy to go to Alaska with his brother Ben. These accounts should become interesting for class sharing.

Interpretive Inquiry

1. Are the Lomans unusual individuals or are they common, everyday people that we all have seen or known?

2. How is the idea of "lostness" brought up time and again in the play? Is Willy the only character who experiences this feeling? How do Biff and Happy fit

into this idea? What of Linda?

3. Why do stockings come up from time to time in the play? What is the author trying to say in contrasting Willy's giving new stockings to the "other woman" and Linda darning her own stockings?

4. Why is Linda shown doing her wash several times during the play? Does this fact have anything to do with the "other woman" in the hotel room?

5. Why does Biff steal things (the football, the fountain pen)? What is the significance of Biff's tendency to steal from others?

6. The play makes quite a thing about the planting of seeds. What does this mean?

7. Willy's older brother Ben appears frequently to speak of striking out for Alaska or Africa. What do these two places represent in the play?

8. Ben repeatedly talks of going into the jungle and coming out rich. What does the jungle mean to Willy? What jungle does he go into (or is he in one)? Which jungle has more potential for riches - Ben's or Willy's?

9. In Act II, Willy talks to Howard about Dave Singleman, who Willy says was a "great salesman." Willy says Singleman died "the death of a salesman." How was Willy's salesmanship different from Singleman's? How was his death different? Is there any significance in naming the two salesman "Loman" and "Singleman"?

10. When Willy learns that Bernard is going to argue a case before the Supreme Court, he is surprised that the boy (Bernard) didn't mention it. And Charley

says, "He don't have to - he's gonna do it." How is this statement ironic with respect to Willy and his two sons?

11. Willy says that Bernard and Charley aren't "well-liked." What does he mean by this? Who does Willy believe to be well-liked? Why? What is the irony in this?

12. Might one conclude that there are two Willy Loman's in this play? If so, how do the two Willys differ?

13. What type of disposition does Biff have? Does he care about his family? His work? Has be fully recovered from the incident he suffered years before in Boston? Why do you think he enjoys ranch work rather than the field of business? How is Biff like Willy? How different? What was Willy's attitude toward people who work with their hands (carpenters, for example)? What prompts this attitude? Why is it extremely ironic?

14. Is Linda primarily a wife or a mother? How does she "mother" Willy? How does she regard her husband? How does her manner toward her husband differ from her manner toward her sons? What is her main concern in life?

15. Do you think Happy has come to better terms with life than his father or brother? How does his success with women affect his personality? Is Happy content? Does he grow as a person in this play? Does he learn anything from Willy's suicide?

16. At the end of the play Happy says he believes Willy's dream was a good one. What did he perceive his

father's dream to be? Is Hap a new Willy?

Intellectual Inquiry

1. Willy Loman scorns people who have trade occupations, yet he is happiest when he is working with his hands. Do you think our society encourages this incongruity, this kind of snobbery? Should everyone be encouraged to strive for the sort of success Bernard has had, or do we place too much importance on going to college to seek professional careers and not enough on other kinds of achievement and success?
2. Can our wanting to do the right things for the people we love lead us into traps? What kinds of things must we know before deciding how to best provide for those we love?
3. Willie stresses the importance of being "well-liked." How important is it to you?
4. How did Willy view his role as a father? What do you think a father's responsibilities are?
5. Did Willy's suicide take more courage than it took to live his life? Are there any circumstances under which you think people have a right to end their lives?
6. Willy's job was his identity, and he becomes, as he says, "Zero" without it. What makes up your identity, your image? What would you like it to be?
7. Where does popularity stand in your value system? Is being well-liked the best criterion for being successful? How do you make people like you? Do you worry about not being well-liked?

8. What kind of relationship do you have with your parents? Do you feel they understand you? Do *you* understand them? How might family members go about trying to understand each other better? Do your parents expect too much of you? Do you ever find yourself trying to spite them? If so, have you ever thought about why you do this?

9. How did Biff feel about financial success? How do *you* feel about it? How do you feel about the emphasis placed on financial success? Are there other kinds of success?

10. How did you feel when you realized Willy was going to kill himself? What did you want to do? What would you have said to Willy if you could have stepped into the play to talk to him? Could you have convinced him to want to continue to live?

11. Willy often looked back on his past. Do you find that you sometimes do the same thing? Why do you look back at past experiences? Do you think it is good to do this? Could it be a bad thing to do?

12. If we are to accept the idea that the world is a jungle and contains both good and bad things, what must we know or what kinds of things must we do to survive in it?

13. Is it better to create an illusory world where one can live quite comfortably, or should one try to cope with hard and unpleasant realities? Which will give a person more satisfaction?

14. Do you have your own value system? Let's try to jot down five values of most importance to us and list them by priority (1, 2, 3). Why have you chosen each

value? Do you think your parents would agree with your list? Why not? How might their priorities differ?

The Glass Menagerie

— Tennessee Williams

Improvisations

1. Before reading the play, have students keep a diary for one week, writing down any daydreams they might have, any thoughts or situations they fantasize about. Have them also jot down their future dreams, anything they are hoping for themselves or someone else. When they bring their thoughts to class, hold a discussion about how almost everyone has dreams and illusions and the extent to which they control our lives.
2. Before reading the play, have students write about a few significant experiences they have had in the past (at any age) that they remember. Begin the session with a discussion on how students know for a fact these experiences actually happened; perhaps they have heard or told the event so many times they only think it happened.
3. Ask students to think about a collection they may have — plants, stuffed animals, etc. Do these seem real to you? Do you talk to them and escape from reality through these objects?
4. Choose one character from the play and predict what he or she is doing five years after the end of the

play. Use the background of the play and the author's interpretation of the characters in the various scenes to defend your predictions. (Good for creative exit from the play.)

5. Dialogue writing and role playing.
   A. Divide class into five groups.
   B. Give each group one of five pre-planned, role-playing situations. (These are listed below.)
   C. Instruct each group to write a dialogue based on their given situation.
   D. When students complete this writing assignment, ask them to select two members from their group to act our their dialogue.
   E. Have students perform their dialogue in front of the class.

Five role-playing situations:

Group one - Amanda and Mr. Wingfield arguing. Explore each personality and why it conflicts with the other. Offer some colorful but realistic dialogue.

Group two - Tom and Mr. Wingfield conversing. Tom and his father run into each other by chance and exchange thoughts and feelings. Are these two similar? How do they feel about leaving Amanda and Laura behind?

Group three - Tom is being fired at the shoe factory. Describe the conversation between him and his boss. How does each of these men feel about "work"?

Group four - Tom and Laura meet years later and discuss whether or not they have been good or kind to their mother. What responsibilities do they feel towards their mother?

Group five - Laura and Jim meet years later. Remarkably so, Laura has transformed into a very attractive, outgoing, and successful young woman. Jim asks her how this new self image emerged and Laura explains. Reflect on how Jim may or may not be responsible for sparking this change.

Interpretive Inquiry

1. Why is this called a "memory play"? Who is untapping the memories? How might the music and lighting contribute to this "memory" style? Does the play seem real or sentimental? Why?
2. Why is the play named *The Glass Menagerie*?
3. What happened to Mr. Wingfield? Why did he go away? Can you blame him?
4. Why is Amanda obsessed with finding a husband for Laura? Isn't Laura capable of finding one herself? Do you think a husband is Laura's only hope? Why or why not?
5. How does Laura react to Rubicam Business College? Why? What does this tell you about her?
6. Why is she so engaged with her glass collection? Is she like her glass ornaments? How does her physical and emotional character resemble these?
7. Jim thinks Laura has an inferiority complex. Do you agree? What personal reasons would she use to construct this complex? Do you think these reasons are justified? Can a complex or lack of confidence stand in the way of a person's happiness or future? How?
8. Does Amanda suffer from a lack of confidence? Compare her with Laura. Which character do you like better? Why?

9. Do you think Amanda is a good mother? Does she love her children? How does she demonstrate love? How do her children react?
10. Why do you think there is a narrator in the play? What function does he serve? Why is Tom the narrator? Why not Laura or Amanda, or Jim?
11. Why does Tom go to the movies so often? What does he mean when he later says, "People go to the movies instead of moving....Hollywood characters are supposed to have all the adventures for everybody in America, while everybody in America sits in a dark room and watches them have them"?
12. What other clues reveal Tom's need for adventure? How does he like working for the Continental Shoe Company? How does he differ from his co-workers? Why does Jim call him Shakespeare?
13. Jim, contrary to the Wingfields, appears quite content with life. Why do you think he is content or happy with his life or himself? How does he view himself?
14. Do you think Jim's encounter with Laura means a great deal to him? What does it mean to Laura? Why is it important to her life?
15. What does Tom mean when he, as narrator, says, "The magician gives you illusion that has the appearance of truth. I give you truth in the pleasant disguise of illusion"?
16. Do you believe Amanda actually had seventeen gentlemen callers one Sunday afternoon? Why do you think she tells the story over and over?
17. Do you think Amanda has actually begun to believe

her own story of seventeen callers, or do you think she knowingly lies to impress others?

18. When Amanda discovers that Laura has not been attending secretarial school, why does she become even more adamant about Laura dating?

19. Throughout the play, why does Amanda continually avoid the fact that Laura is crippled?

20. Why does Tom get so upset when Amanda returns his book by D.H. Lawrence to the library?

21. How and why does Tom shatter Laura's glass collection? What are Laura's and Tom's reactions?

22. One evening when Tom returns from a movie, he tells Laura that he saw a magician escape from a nailed coffin. Why is this incident significant to Tom's character?

23. After one evening meal, Amanda offers to bring the dessert to the table and says to Laura, "You be the lady this time and I'll be the darky." How does this comment characterize Amanda?

24. Why is Laura's figure spotlighted throughout the third scene quarrel between Tom and Amanda?

25. Under stress, Laura plays with objects which represent "all the softest emotions that belong to recollections of things past." What are they?

26. Why does Amanda carry a bunch of jonquils and wear a girlish dress on the night Jim O'Connor comes to call?

27. Right after Laura opens the door for Jim, why does she rush across the room to her phonograph?

28. What significance does the unicorn in the glass collection have?

29. Why does Laura give the broken unicorn to Jim after he tells her of his engagement?
30. Why does Amanda blame Tom for the evening's failure?
31. Why did it take Tom so long to leave home?
32. Like his mother, Tom had dreams and illusions, but he seemed to know the real world. What was real to him?
33. Does Tom really care for his sister? Does he ever regret having to leave her?
34. Do you think Laura fully understands her own position and the responsibility that Tom feels for her?
35. What does the impact of Jim's engagement announcement cause Amanda to recognize about herself and her whole family?
36. What meaning about the past does Williams suggest by having Laura blow out the candles as Tom says good bye?
37. What guesses might one make about the characters' destinies? Which character's life looks most promising? Why?

Intellectual Inquiry

1. Why is there disharmony in the Wingfield home? What produces this in a family? Is it the financial struggle or the emotional tension between family members? What else can it be?
2. Who is responsible for Tom and Amanda's constant fighting? Does either person try to understand the other's viewpoint? Do they listen to each other? Why do you think it's important to listen to other

people? Is it possible to understand people better by being a better listener?

3. Do you think Tom is justified in leaving home? What would make you want to leave home?

4. What kind of expecatations do parents have of their children? Do you think children can or should always live up to these expectations? Why or why not? Does this apply to your expectations of parents as well?

5. Laura has a poor self image. How does your self image affect the quality of your life? Is there a way to change or improve your self image?

6. In the last scene of the play Jim encourages Laura to believe in herself. He states, "Everybody excels in some one thing....all you've got to do is discover in what." Do you agree with Jim? Does everybody have one special quality?

7. Because of a childhood disease Laura has to wear a brace on her leg. Does she let this "small defect" govern her life? Jim says her handicap is "magnified thousands of times" by her imagination. Would you agree with him? Do you sometimes magnify yours or others' small imperfections? How does society treat people with handicaps? How do you feel about this?

8. Do you think the characters, Amanda, Tom, and Laura, take responsibility for their own lives without placing great importance on their present or past circumstances? Is it sometimes easier to blame *circumstances* instead of accepting personal responsibility for your life?

9. Do these characters exhibit control over their lives?

Do you feel you have control over your life? Why or why not?

10. Do you think it's possible for someone to believe something strongly enough to convince himself or herself it is real?

11. Do you think you can avoid the truth by simply not talking about it?

12. Have you ever felt that your parents are trying to fulfill their own lives and to rectify mistakes they made in the past by reliving through you and/or your brothers and sisters? Does this get in the way of doing what YOU want?

13. Do you know anyone who tried to get you to conform to his or her idea of behavior rather than letting you assert your own personality? Do you do this to others?

14. What tangible objects or possessions do you have that might give you a feeling of security? Do you turn to them when you feel nervous or insecure?

15. Have you ever wanted to believe something so badly that you talked yourself and others into an illusion of reality?

16. Have you ever contemplated running away from your structured and sheltered environment? Do you know anyone who has? Do you think running away can solve whatever problems you may have?

17. Do you know anyone with similar characteristics as Amanda? Can you admire her perseverance and understand what motivates her, or do you merely consider her a silly, frustrated woman?

Index